Far
Vo

BEDFORD BUSES
OF THE
1970S AND 1980S

Alan Earnshaw

with

Michael P. Berry
&
Martin Eltham

NOSTALGIA ROAD PUBLICATIONS

CONTENTS

INTRODUCTION	3
FROM THE 1960s TO THE 1970s	4
BEDFORD BUS & COACH DESIGNATIONS	7
A NEW ERA - THE YRQ	12
THE 11-METRE YRTs	16
THE SB LIVES ON (THE NFM / NJM)	19
THE VERSATILE VAS (PJK)	22
COLOUR FILES	25
MICRO MAGIC (THE CF SERIES)	29
AN OLD FAVOURITE - THE TJ SERIES	32
MOVING ON - THE YLQ/YMP SERIES	34
THE YMT SERIES	37
A NEW GENERATION?	40
LAST ENDEAVOURS (YNT SERIES)	42
A FINAL VENTURE (THE YNV SERIES)	45
END OF AN ERA	47
TRUCK-DERIVED BUSES	48
TESTING TIMES	50

The **Nostalgia Road** Series ™

is produced under licence by

Nostalgia Road Publications Ltd.

Unit 6, Chancel Place

Shap Road Industrial Estate, Kendal LA9 6NZ

Tel. 01539 738832 - Fax: 01539 730075

designed and published by
Trans-Pennine Publishing Ltd.
PO Box 10, Appleby-in-Westmorland, Cumbria, CA16 6FA
Tel. 017683 51053 Fax. 017683 53558
e-mail: admin@transpenninepublishing.co.uk

and printed by
Kent Valley Colour Printers Ltd.
Kendal, Cumbria
01539 741344

© Trans-Pennine Publishing Ltd. 2003
Photographs: Vauxhall Motors or as credited

Front Cover: *This 45-seat Bedford YRQ with a Plaxton Elite body carries a promotional registration plate (PLA 71 - for Plaxton 1971) and is finished in the livery of Valliant Silverline*

Rear Cover Top: *Purchased new by Thomas Coaches of South Wales in the autumn of 1981, MAX 331X is a Bedford VAS with a C29F 'shortened' Plaxton Paramount body. In this publicity picture the owner takes his latest acquisition up in to the Brecon Beacons for the Vauxhall publicity photographer. The VAS chassis may have dated back to the early 1960s, but it remained a popular small coach right down to the end at Bedford.*

Rear Cover Bottom: *Premier of Cambridge introduced PRE 1M, a stylish Duple Dominant MkI body on a YRT chassis in 1973. Behind it can be seen a YRQ with a Willowbrook service bus body.*

Title Page: *Two YRT chassis are seen with different styles of bodywork; on the left is the Willowbrook Spacecar on test with the NBC, on the right (KUR 239P) a Bedford demonstrator with Plaxton body - see pages 16-18.*

This Page: *After two decades in production, the VAS had become the PJK; here a Reeve Burgess B17F body is fitted. See pages 22-24.*

INTRODUCTION

Following on from my first book in this series, which described the "birth" of Bedford buses and their development through the 1930s and '40s, the boom years of the 1950s and '60s was covered by Michael Berry. We now complete the trilogy with this long-awaited overview of Bedford Buses in the 1970s and '80s with the assistance of Martin Eltham of Darlington.

The 1970s remained high-rolling years, but the 1980s would signal the end of an era, for halfway through the decade, the Bedford Marque was suddenly and dramatically to come to an end as part of the General Motors product range. After a spell as an independent GM subsidiary, Bedford and the plant at Dunstable were sold off to David Brown (not he of Aston Martin and tractor fame), but the entrepreneurial owner of what could have been a successful continuation of a remarkable product range. Sadly Brown and AWD were not to prove up to the job, and a world-leading manufacturer and its brand name fizzled quietly off the scene in 1991.

Promises of a revival under the Marshalls of Cambridge banner came to nothing and the flame finally spluttered out in 1999. Hopes for some kind of a revival by ERF might have come after they acquired millions of parts from Marshall SPV, but the Cheshire manufacturers have had more than enough problems of their own in recent times and the Bedford spares service was sold on to Autoflow.

Above: *Fitted with grant (twin-leaf) doors, BNO 886T was a YMT chassis with a Duple Dominant II C53F body, and was No.1200 in the fleet of the NBC subsidiary Eastern National.*

So we are left with the history, but what a great story that is. This book will tell the latter part of that story, thanks mainly to official photos supplied by Vauxhall Motors. To this end, we owe a debt of thanks to Stuart Harris, Dennis Sherer and Peter Stone at Vauxhall.

Although it would be nice to have a neat time frame in which to describe the company's product range, the actual products themselves rarely oblige by fitting neatly into the start and finish dates of these periods. Therefore, we have to start the account of the 1970s with a range of products that were put into production earlier in the 1960s or, in the case of the SB, back in the 1950s.

This narrative presupposes that the reader will have already studied the two earlier books, as there simply is not the space in this volume to cover that ground again. Even so, it is an interesting journey, and one with which Martin Eltham was personally involved (his step-father was a sales rep for Plaxton coach-builders). This is a story about which all three contributors have real enthusiasm, some of which will hopefully rub off as you read the pages that follow

Alan Earnshaw

Appleby-in-Westmorland
August 2003

FROM THE 1960s TO THE 1970s

It would be easy to start this narrative with a blank sheet of paper, but history does not readily oblige, as Bedford's start to the 1970s was marked by a variety of models from previous decades that were still in production; notably the SB chassis which had started life in 1950 as a replacement for the OB.

Of course the capacity of the SB had increased from its initial 33-seats, and there were significant engine changes as well; but it was still in regular production albeit designated as the NFM/NJM. With its 300 cu. inch petrol engine or the reliable 330 cu. inch diesel, it went on to become the most popular UK bus chassis ever built with approaching 58,000 made in a 35-year period (see page 19).

The VAM had been a logical development of the SB, giving a PSV chassis with the entry doors ahead of the front axle. It had been influenced by a controversial development by the Loughborough coachbuilders W. S. Yeates, who had (in answer to operational needs) stuck a front-end chassis extension on to the SB to permit true front-entrance and one-man-operation. The VAM, designed by Leo Taylor, had been Bedford's response, but it was to be short-lived as a new generation of under-floor-engined PSV chassis would appear with the YRQ series.

Above: *This YRQ / Plaxton demonstrator, a DP45F was prepared for the 1972 Commercial Motor Show. The window sticker reads dual purpose body £6,557.50, YRQ chassis £2,595.50; which was presumably a show price as it does not agree with list prices.*

The first VAMs had a choice of three engines, these being the 300 cu. inch (4.93-litre) Bedford petrol engine in the VAM3 and the 330 cu. inch (5.42-litre) Bedford diesel in the VAM5; both of which had six-cylinders. Based on the successful application of the 401 cu. inch Leyland diesel in the VAL14, the same engine was available on this chassis as the VAM14. Therefore the real change came with Bedford's decision to dump the Leyland power units previously fitted to the VAM and VAL, and fit their own 6-cylinder, 466 cu. inch (7.634-litre) diesel engine.

This new engine, launched at the 1966 Commercial Motor Show, fed the transmission through a close-ratio 5-speed gearbox. The traditional front-mounted radiator was replaced by an under-floor unit. This radiator was fitted just ahead of the engine in a slightly 'tipped' position as opposed to being fitted in the perpendicular, as it was thought that this would give greater protection. Stone damage during tests of the prototype led to the fitting of screen flaps, due to the amount of 'gunge' thrown up by the front wheels.

Top Right: *A picture that could well be entitled VAMs inside and out, as here we have an excellent image taken to portray the very first pair of Continental-bodied buses to appear on the British coach market. This view is strictly before our time period for this book, as it was taken in 1969. However, when Moseley's introduced the bodies from Caetano of Portugal, they did so using the VAM chassis. This view clearly shows the distinctive external styling of the Caetano Cascais and also the way the VAM engine protruded into the bus body.*

Bottom Right: *A Vauxhall styling department drawing of a VAM chassis laid out to a B39/40D arrangement for a municipal operator application. It was envisaged that this arrangement could be applied to Marshall, Willowbrook or Eastern Counties styling. W. Cherry*

Meanwhile, the VAM still had a lot of life left, and as its market place was by no means exhausted, it was re-launched as the VAM 70 in 1968. Considered to be the logical successor to the SB, the VAM really did fit the role that many operators wanted, namely that of both a front line excursion / private hire coach and also a stage carriage bus. The arrangement with the entry doors ahead of the front axle was perfect for one-man-operation, and the front passenger seat alongside the driver no longer caused a distraction; this could be a real problem when the passengers were raucous school children, complaining grannies going shopping, or long-legged girls in very short mini-skirts.

Even so, the VAM wasn't everyone's cup of tea, especially in rural areas where a 7' 6" body was required, as the chassis could only take an 8' wide body. Yet it did have its adherents, even in rural areas and it was well-liked in parts of Scotland where it was employed by operators like Highland Omnibus and Eastern Scottish. It enjoyed an active role in many different guises, including luxury coach, dual-purpose bus and service bus, as well as seeing a few developed for non-PSV uses such as mobile libraries, blood transfusion units and racehorse transporters.

The active marketing of the VAM for the UK domestic market came to an end in 1971, as buyers were pointed towards the newer and more expensive YRQ; yet the VAM did not disappear altogether!

Although the YRQ would eventually take over Bedford's British mid-market range, the VAM would continue to sell in reasonable export quantities. The reason for this was the feeling that in many countries, including Australia, India, New Zealand and Pakistan the roads were often 'unmade' or in too poor a condition for an under-floor engined bus. Stones thrown up from such a surface would readily damage the radiator, and the engine and gearbox casings weren't immune either. As the export market for Bedford buses was quite a sizeable one, it made sense to keep the VAM alive as a front-entrance, normal engine layout for the overseas customer.

In this form it was marketed as the BLP, and duly fitted with an 8.2-litre engine. Substantial numbers were sold in Completely Knocked Down (CKD) kit form and sent to Australasia; where many were built by the body builders Commonwealth Air. In its BLP form the VAM remained moderately successful, and therefore stayed in production until 1985 albeit in small numbers.

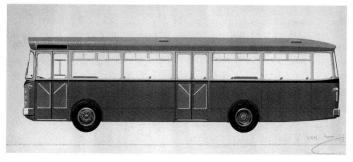

Top Left: *This is believed to be the prototype VAL chassis fitted with the 466 engine, therefore making it a VAL70. Attention was also paid to the brakes on this prototype, as the brakes on the VAL14 had tended to overheat and crack as a result. Regretfully the test reports for this chassis are missing from the records.*

Middle Left: *This batch of VAL14s were swiftly recalled once they had entered service with Trans World Airlines airport buses and fitted with the 466 engine, therefore making them VAL70s - note the central doors on these large capacity people carriers.*

Bottom Left: *Amongst the last of the VAL70s to be built, CAR 433K was new to Perth Coaches, who entered it in the 19th Coach Rally.*

Two other main model types were still in production at the start of the 1970s, the VAS dating from 1961 (see page 22) and the VAL14 (from 1962). Both needed something of a face-lift for the new decade, but the VAL had rapidly become established as the nation's most inexpensive maximum capacity coach, offering capacities in the 45- to 53-seat arena. Initially fitted with the Leyland 400 engine, the VAL14 had seen progressive changes and carried a wide variety of body makes, although Duple and Plaxton were the two most popular builders.

At the end of 1967 Bedford up-rated the VAL14, and in its stead they introduced the new VAL70, which (like the new VAM 70) gained the 466 cu inch engine. (The last of the VAL14s seems to have been bodied early in 1968). With the Leyland engine replaced by an 'in-house' power unit, one might have thought that the VAL 70 would have gone on from strength to strength, but conversely two developments would sound its death-knell. First of all we have the move to the under-floor concept started by the VAM, followed by Bedford's assessment of the changing market place following the 1968 Transport Act and changes in the Construction & Use Regulations.

Those 16-inch wheels that had given the VAL such a major success due to its low loading height could now be substituted by other innovations and at the same time designers could get around the awkward staggered entry steps on the chassis.

The subject of the VAL's demise will be told in a forthcoming book from Nostalgia Road, but suffice it to say that one of the country's best-loved coach chassis was to have a short life in its VAL70 guise, ending production in 1973; the last chassis to leave Dunstable being No.2T474319 (GAT 502L) fitted with a Plaxton C53F body that went new to Danby of Hull (4/73). Bodies used on the VAL70 were mostly Plaxton Elite and Duple Viceroy, but not exclusively so; meanwhile quite a number of the VAL70s continued the tradition of the earlier models in use for non-PSV applications.

The VAL in both forms therefore only had a manufacturing spell of around a decade, but it remains an enduring favourite with operators and enthusiasts alike, and in its 40th year, the model featured strongly at the Bedford Gathering in August 2002. No less than 18 of the 25 examples that are preserved were present, but in total around 57 VAL14s and 62 VAL70s are known to survive at the time of writing.

THE BEDFORD PSV CHASSIS DESIGNATIONS

For many enthusiasts, the most significant change in the Bedford bus and coach chassis range was the new set of designations that appeared (seemingly) overnight and caused much confusion amongst enthusiasts and operators alike.

Previously the model designations on Bedford PSV chassis had all been derived directly from the truck ranges and were designated by the addition of a 'B' to the truck model designation, thus the WHB, WLB, WTB, OB, OWB, and SB, were the bus versions of the WH, WL, WT, O, OW and S series trucks. Only the J-Types and the new VA series (VAS, VAM and VAL) from the 1960s differed from this philosophy. As a consequence, it became relatively easy to chart the progress of the Bedford Marque, although some readers have asked what designations like TJ2 stood for. Simplistically the answer is T= truck, J = series or type, 2 - 2-tons, and so on!

Less easily understood are the suffixes that followed the chassis code, especially on the SB model. But again, it is quite simple really, for as the availability of engine options increase, the suffix letter G or O (initially used to indicate Gasoline or Oil engines) on the SB chassis became inadequate.

Above: A Bedford YRT with a Willowbrook Warrior body is seen in service with Red Rose Travel at Watlington in 1992. Although it gained its Certificate of Fitness in October 1998, it seems odd that a 12-year old YRT subject to normal wear and tear would have been worth bodying. The DVLA were obviously not sure of its year of manufacture at the time of its registration, hence Q956 UOE. However, the chassis number (GC254979ZOFW) helps us to identify it as being manufactured in 1976 at Dunstable with a temporary drive-away front end. From this we can tell it went to Willowbrook, where it was originally fitted with a Spacecar body, and as NFP 735P was used as a team coach by Nottinghamshire County Cricket Club. Malcolm Knight

The new engine suffix arrangement was: -.

1	=	Bedford 300 cu. in. Diesel
2	=	Bedford 214 cu. in. Petrol
3	=	Bedford 300 cu. in. Petrol
5	=	Bedford 330 cu. in. Diesel
8	=	Leyland 350 cu. in. Diesel
13	=	Leyland 370 cu. in. Diesel
14	=	Leyland 401 cu. in. Diesel

Top Left: *The Bedford VAS was originally fitted with the 300 cu. inch diesel engine (VAS1) or the 214 cu. inch petrol engine (VAS2), but the advent of the 330 cu. inch diesel engine made a significant improvement in what became the VAS5. Later designated the PJK, the 330 engine powers this 29-seat staff transport bus for the BBC, which is fitted with a Duple Dominant body.*

Middle Left: *It was extremely rare to find Bedford coaches in municipal fleets, but one big exception was Edinburgh City Transport who had a sizeable fleet from this maker, including VAM, VAL and YRQ models. In this August 1973 picture, part of the fleet is seen at rest, with several VAMs behind YRQ VSC 421J.* Alan Earnshaw

Bottom Left: *The stunning good looks of the Plaxton body on the VAL70 made a combination hard to beat. Here, seen to great effect, is FLG 630K, which was new to E. J. Bostock & Sons as their fleet number 19 and shown at the 18th British Coach Rally, Brighton.*

With the first of the non-truck derived bus chassis in the 1960s a new series was started i.e. the VA range, but now an additional letter was necessary to indicate wheelbase length; S, M, and L, for short, medium and long respectively. Coupled with the suffix designations, we end up with the new model type; for example, VAL14, VAM5 and VAS2. Later Bedford's own 466-cu.in diesel engine replaced the Leyland engines in the VAL and VAM resulting in models VAL70 and VAM70. At the same time the use of Leyland engines in the SB was also discontinued.

In 1968, new model indications came about with the introduction of computer scheduling and parts listing, although for a long while the old familiar names continued to be used in "Sales talk" and reference to SB and VAL never really died out. However, to explain the new system, I am indebted to the following information supplied by Leo Taylor of Dunstable, formerly a senior engineer with Bedford's bus division The new system consisted of a seven-character "alpha numeric" code, in which each character specified a particular feature of the vehicle concerned, for example, take the VAS which became the PJK;

	P	J	K	1	B	ZO
Model Line.	*					
Engine.		*				
GVW Group*			*			
Wheelbase range				*		
Drive Line.					*	
Cab Type						*

* Gross Vehicle Weight

As the truck ranges were more comprehensive than the buses, the system had more capacity than was necessary to differentiate the bus variants. For instance with an increase of a bus chassis wheelbase came a larger bus with more passenger space and therefore an increase in Gross Vehicle Weight was needed, but the same was not true with the trucks. In any single bus line uniqueness would be defined by either wheelbase or GVW, both were not required.

In this system new model indications were generated as follows;
The first character indicated the model line: -

N	Formerly SB
P	Formerly VAS
T	Formerly VAM. (T was subsequently altered to B)
W	Formerly VAL
Y	The new mid-engined range

The second character, indicating the engine, was selected from the following: -

O	All engines appropriate to the model line	
D	214 cu. in. Petrol	formally number 2
F	300 cu. in. Petrol	formally number 3
J	330 cu. in. Diesel	formally number 5
R	466 cu. in. Diesel	formally number 70
L	8.2 litre Diesel	de-rated to 110 kW power
M	8.2 litre Diesel	119 kW power or T/C to 130 kW
N	8.2 litre Diesel	Turbo charged to 153 kW power

The third character indicates the group of GVW's into which chassis designed gross weight falls, in the case of the buses these were: -

O	all appropriate G.V.W.	
K	approx.	7,000kg
M	approx.	9,900kg
P	approx.	10,400kg
Q	approx.	11,400kg
T	approx.	13,000kg
V	max.	16,000kg

The fourth character indicated the wheelbase group thus: -

O	all appropriate wheelbases
1	short wheelbase
2	medium wheelbase
3	long wheelbase
4	extra long wheelbase

Top Right: *An August 1972 pictureof a YRQ taken at Seamer Road Scarborough, with Plaxton's new demonstrator for 1973; at 32' 6" by 8' 2.5" it had a maximum capacity of 45-seats, but 43-, 41-, and 38-seat options could also be specified. Known as the Panorama Elite II, it had a body price of £5,610. Optional extras could include a HMV radio system, four speakers and microphone at £103.00, air-operated door gear at £110.00, sorbo-rubber flooring in place of lino £69.00, spring-loaded nylon nets to rear of seats £2.75 each, armrests at £5.50 each, or fog/spot lamps at £12.00 each. Plaxton Ltd.*

Bottom Right: *Also from 1972, another Elite II body, this time a 53-seater on the YRT chassis poses near Neath, South Wales. In the livery of Cream Line Services Ltd., Tonmawr, NNY 637L is seen just above the village of Pontrhydyfen, which was the birthplace of the actor, Richard Burton. A colour image of this vehicle is found on page 25.*

Top Left: *Chassis like the SB and the VAS continued to be used for applications like mobile libraries and welfare buses right down to the end. This 1986 PJK was fitted with a Wright body and supplied to the London Borough of Lambeth, where it was used as a 'Consumerbus' for training people from foreign countries about their rights.* Wrightbus

Middle Left: *On the Vauxhall test track, we see a YRQ with a Willowbrook Expressway DP45F body. It looks a stylish coach, but the windows on these bodies tend to 'bake' the passengers in hot weather, and windscreens also had a nasty habit of falling out.*

Bottom Left: *One of a batch of chassis supplied to Arlington Motors as stock, NNK 808P was given a Dominant service bus body and sold to the Atomic Research Establishment. After service at Harwell it went to Hopley's and is seen here in Truro in 1996.* Alan Earnshaw

The fifth character defined the transmission and rear axle as follows: -

O	all appropriate options
B	4 speed gearbox/single speed axle
D	5 speed gearbox/single speed axle
V	6 speed overdrive gearbox/single speed axle
N	6 speed direct drive gearbox/single speed axle

The final two characters define the "Body style" as applied to a chassis. In the case of the bus chassis, bodywork was restricted to that necessary to enable the chassis to be driven short distances prior to mounting of the bus/coach body, the chassis in this state was not "Road Legal". Body options were: -

OO	all appropriate options
ZO	temporary drive-away front end
EO	drive-away front end with mostly permanent content

As was stated earlier the range of bus chassis was limited and whilst use of the full code was essential in some circumstances it was normally only necessary to use the first three characters and this became the norm, i.e. PJK, NJM, TRP, BLP, YRQ, YMT, and YNV.

The reason for all the zeros lay in the parts listing and production scheduling so that any part that was used on every variant in a model line irrespective of engine, gross weight, wheelbase, drive line or body style, for example, the steering wheel, would appear in the schedules for use on model YOOOOOO, sometimes shortened to a single Y, instead of having to list every variant against the single part number. These forms were not generally used outside the parts lists of schedules. The 12-metre YNV chassis was the only Bedford bus chassis to have a model name and was badged "VENTURER".

Chassis numbers or Vehicle Identification Number, (VIN) were comprised of the seven character model indication plus a letter denoting the year of manufacture, e.g. A= 1971, B= 1972, etc. and a further letter identifying the General Motors plant of origin, i.e. W for Dunstable. The following six digit numbers were not unique to the model line but were allotted to the frames.

As they started on the final assembly conveyor, which contained a mixture of truck and bus chassis, the consecutive numbers could be TJ, TK or M type trucks or any of the bus models. A typical VIN would be YRQ2DZODW456789, representing a chassis built in 1974. As a result of the dealer and bodybuilder stocking procedures and bodybuilding time scales it could be many months, and in extreme cases years, before the chassis was bodied and completed and placed into service.

In the early 1980s in accordance with new international regulations some changes became necessary. The use of the letters Q and O was banned, so model YMQ became YMP and the 7th character of the model indication was dropped. At the same time the letters SKF were added to identify the manufacturer and country of origin, the plant designator was changed from W to T and a new sequence of date letters was started, thus a typical VIN became SKFYNT3VZCT123456.

Above: *In contrast to the YMTs opposite, this one (RRC 199R) had a more functional Willowbrook B52F body for use as miner's transport. This one went to Worksop in the NCB South Notts Area.*

It was in this form, without spaces, that the number was embossed on the VIN plate along with the series of three digit numbers specifying the Regular Production Options built into the chassis; example: - 180 = Heavy Duty Rear Suspension or 501 = Automatic Transmission. When the VIN was stamped on the chassis side-member two extra asterisks were added to prevent unauthorised alterations viz.; * SKFYNT3VZCT123456 *

So, despite what the press of the day had to say, it wasn't a case of 'think of a number', it was a logical, well thought-out alpha-numeric solution to the needs of computerised management; the only true problem lay in the fact that Bedford didn't really explain it all that well to the average enthusiast!

A New Era - The YRQ

As stated previously, the changes allowed by the Construction & Use Regulations gave rise to new opportunities for the UK coach chassis builders. Perhaps the first manufacturer to make a really significant change was Robert Seddon Ltd, in Oldham, for with their new Seddon-Pennine RU they took the British PSVs into new territory. The most significant change of the period was the new ground clearance regulations, and the RU took full advantage of these. We mention Seddon at this point, because although they were not newcomers to the bus market, they did burst into the market in a big way in the 1970s, specifically aiming to succeed in a market place that had been dominated by the lower-cost chassis makers like Bedford, Commer and Ford.

The low ground clearance offered by the 16-inch wheels on the VAS and VAL had given Bedford an advantage in the 1960s, but the new regulations actually made the company fair game for the competition. The VAS would remain safe, but it was the front-entrance VAM and VAL that were the most likely casualties in the product war that was about to emerge.

Above: *Used for sight-seeing tours in the Scottish capital this 1971 YRQ (VSC 241J) had a Duple Viceroy C45F body, and was no 241 in the Edinburgh City Transport fleet.*

The big drawback with the VAM and the VAL were the narrow, and painfully restricted entrances, which featured a set of dog-leg steps and were therefore not the most convenient means of entry or exit. The fact that the engine cowl protruded into the body also made the driving position less than comfortable, and like the Ford R226 chassis of the same era it hemmed the driver into his driving position, and radiated a fair amount of heat towards his legs; this was ideal for cold winter morning school runs, but awful when crawling into Blackpool on a Bank Holiday Monday morning.

One-man-operation of the VAM, whilst entirely feasible, was still hampered by the big, broad lump that separated the driver and the entry steps. Moving to the under-floor concept was the logical answer, and Bedford's new Y-Series would both revolutionise the company's market place, and also provide an economical alternative to the traditional expensive under-floor-engine chassis such as AEC, Leyland and so on.

The YRQ would therefore change four decades of Bedford tradition, as no longer would they employ their standard mechanical practice of a front-fitted engine driving the rear axle by means of a clutch, gearbox and prop-shaft. This arrangement had previously led to quite high noise levels, due to the fact that the engine came right into the front of the passenger area, despite sound-deadening material and plush moquette covers being fitted to the cowls. This situation would remain on the SB (NJM) and VAS (PJK) models, where the cowls would remain directly between the front passenger seats and the driver.

Oddly enough the genesis for the YRQ, and therefore the beginning of the end for the VAM was largely down to one man, their senior PSV engineer Leo Taylor. Following the problematic FE44/SB from Yeates, he had been given the responsibility of developing the VAM concept for Bedford, and there is no doubt that he successfully introduced one of the most interesting, if little-discussed developments in Bedford's long PSV history. Yet the fact remains that the VAM did not replace the SB, as some had anticipated, and the traditionalists would ensure that the bus that started off life as the 'Big Bedford' would last into the 1980s as the country's most popular 'small coach' chassis.

However, neither was the VAM taken out of circulation straight away, for it would remain available as an export model for some time. Yet for the home market, Bedford actively developed the YRQ, the designation for which represented: -

    Y = Mid-engine range,
    R = 466 cu. inch Diesel Engine
    Q = approx 11,400kg.

After extensive trials, in which the prototype chassis was carried under a Duple Viceroy 37 body (YXE 844H) the new YRQ chassis was launched in September 1970. Photographs taken of the prototype at this time were labelled as the VAM70, and so successful were they in disguising the real chassis, that we inadvertently captioned YXE 844H on the rear cover of *Bedford Buses of the 1950s and '60s* as a VAM70. Our apologies for this error, but the subterfuge of the 1970 picture fooled us all 30 years on.

Top Right: *To right the wrong, we show another view of YXE 844H, which is fitted with a Duple Viceroy body - a type that had been widely employed on the Bedford VAM and the Ford R226. It was one of the first designs to be made by Duple when they transferred production from Hendon to the former Burlingham works at Vicarage Road in Blackpool. The standard of the bodywork on the Viceroy was not, however, up to that employed on the Vega series. Hardwood was replaced by marine ply, and the durability of the bodies seemed suspect. Alan Earnshaw is currently overcoming some of these problems on his Viceroy 37.*

Bottom Right: *In this third view of YXE 844H, we have an excellent interior image showing the positioning of the 466 cu. inch under-floor engine with the access hatch lifted. Beyond this hatch, the battery compartment is also seen. A drawback to this arrangement was that dirty hands could easily soil the seating moquette.*

Top Left: *Obviously with just two major British players left in the luxury coach building market by the 1970s, the choice was limited. Here is the first YRQ Panorama Elite II demonstrator pictured at the back of the Scarborough factory in 1970. For service bus requirements, Plaxton offered the Derwent body for the YRQ chassis.*

Middle Left: *This YRQ (UWX 914L) is a very early example of the new Duple Dominant coach body, and was new to John S. Powell of Rotherham.* Andrew Webster

Bottom Left: *In contrast GHN 858N is a YRQ with a Dominant B47F service bus body. It was new to Cleveland Transit as fleet no. 358 in 1974, but in 1984 the body was shortened and reduced in capacity to a B35F.*

The first YRQ was bodied by Duple, but Plaxton also had a major share in the coach market, placing bodies of up to 45-seats on the 193-inch wheelbase. The reviews of the YRQ were mixed, and it has to be said that at first some did not really see Bedford as an under-floor engine contender against the might of the British Leyland Group (BL). However, almost all the reviews were unanimous, and they all commented on the fact that the new arrangement was significantly quieter than the conventional Bedford design.

The YRQ may not have been a true contender when compared to the Leopard or Reliance chassis from BL, but they were substantially cheaper. A significant factor in reducing the cost was the fact that Taylor and his team carried over many components from the VAM chassis. This was not only very cost effective for Bedford and their dealers, but also for those operators who carried large stocks of Bedford parts. Of course it was the heart of the beast that mattered, and transferring the 466 cu. inch unit from the VAM70 / VAL 70 was a distinct compromise; indeed it was this element that gave some reviewers their only concerns about the YRQ's overall performance. As it was, it would not be until the mid-1970s that a more powerful Bedford power unit would be used on the YRQ and its larger sister the YRT.

In terms of its chassis, the new YRQ was basically a modified VAM, a fact that can be determined by the wheelbase and the front / rear chassis overhang. Drive was still to the rear axle by means of a prop-shaft, albeit shorter than that on the VAM, and final drive was via a fully-floating hypoid type of rear axle. The brakes were substantially improved and benefited from an increased lining area of 652 square inches. The earlier VAM had a brake lining area of 600 square inches and had been known to suffer from 'fading' problems. One operator from Consett told us he had this experience first-hand, having taken a Plaxton-bodied VAM down the B6278 at Crawleyside in Weardale when it was about nine-years-old. He recalls 'There had been a bad accident with a coach on this road in the 1950s, and safety sand drags had been installed as a consequence. Coming down towards Stanhope, the brakes on my 1969-built VAM began to fade badly, and I had no alternative but to put her into the sand-drag, breaking two front leaf springs in the process - but better that than..........!!!!

But the thing that really caught me out was the modified engine sump! Having cracked the sump as well as the springs, I decided that I would swap over the engine as a complete unit, as we had a 466 cu. inch unit brand new and still in its original case in the workshop; what I had not reckoned on was the fact that this had been bought for (but not used) on a Plaxton-bodied VAM a few years previously. Out came the original unit and up was offered the replacement, but it didn't fit, as the sump casing had been modified to facilitate the new under-floor engine position! In fact there were a few subtle changes to the engine, including an improved crankcase, a modified fan and a reduction in noise levels, mind you, compared to the VAM, getting second gear on our YRQs could be a devil of a job.'

At this time Plaxton were actively involved in promoting the YRQ with the Derwent service bus body, and they particularly tried to get customers to go for the Dual-Purpose specification, as the more comfortable seating meant that the resulting vehicle could be equally at home on stage-carriage and excursion work. Oddly enough, Pennine Coachworks at Oldham were making similar claims for the Seddon RU, and Bristol / ECW were going for the same market place with their models.

One owner from Shropshire recalled that 'there was a significant hike in the chassis price of the YRQ, which at just over £2,000 was £350 more than the VAM; but this *was* a time of significant inflation. Our Plaxton-bodied YRQs weighed in at just under 7-tons and I think the Duple's were perhaps 2- to 3-cwt or so less, so the overall weight was slightly less than the VAM, and this marginally helped to give a slightly better fuel consumption'. Our previous volume showed pictures of the VAM 70s bought by Scottish Omnibuses Ltd, in 1968, but the former SMT group went over to the Bristol LH for its next big batch of orders in 1970. The YRQ's advent changed the situation back in Bedford's favour and the next big batch of 50 service coach orders (all Alexander-bodied) specified the YRQ chassis. Yet it was with the small independent operators that the YRQ became truly popular, and on the basis of this success it became Britain's top-selling bus / coach chassis with around 656 examples entering service in 1972 alone.

Top Right: *This was Plaxton's Derwent service bus body, but at 37-seats, it represents one of the low-seating / high-standing capacity arrangements. New in 1974, SYO 601N went to Golden Miller of Feltham.*

Middle Right: *Following on from its batches of VAM / Alexander orders in the late 1960s, Scottish Omnibuses returned to Bedford after trying the Bristol LH. Here we see Eastern Scottish YC574A (SFS 574N) with Alexander bodywork.*

Bottom Right: *The advent of the YRQ in the NBC subsidiary fleets was something of a puzzle too, but along with its big sister (the YRT) some decent orders were received. Here we see United Counties No.195, another 1974 model but this time carrying Willowbrook/BET B45F bodywork; it is finished in NBC leaf green.*

THE 11-METRE YRTs

With the aforementioned changes in the Construction & Use Regulations, Bedford announced that the VAL70 would be withdrawn and replaced by the new YRT that they would launch in June 1972. Like the YRQ, the YRT would employ an under-floor engine using the modified 4.66cu. inch power plant. This chassis would however aim at the 11-metre, 51-53 seat market, and the designation stood for: -

    Y = Under-floor range
    R = 466 cu. inch diesel engine
    T = approx 13,000kg gross vehicle weight

One dealer/operator from South Yorkshire told us 'The longer (222-inch) wheelbase seemed an ideal contender for the 'big coach' field, but I honestly had my doubts that the YRTs 136bhp could be a reasonable challenge to the AEC, Leyland or new Volvo chassis that I drove. I recall delivering a YRT to an operator in Barnstaple in 1973, and after leaving Taunton, I found the steep banks of the Somerset and Devon hills quite a challenge, even with an empty coach. In my regular work around the Pennines, especially with a load of miners on an early morning wintertime run, I cursed the lack of power more often than I complimented the smooth ride.'

Above: *Barton Transport of Chilwell, found the grant-specification YRTs ideal for dual purpose work; as they used them on both stage carriage services and private hire / excursion duties. Here fleet No.1303 (WRR 341M) carries Duple Dominant C53F bodywork.*

The YRT design was built to a quite heavy-duty specification, and it therefore employed many components from the TK and KM truck range. A rugged 5-speed Eaton gearbox was standard, as to (thankfully) was power-assisted steering and an air-assisted clutch. Even so, it was still a big brute, and at approaching 8-tons it was a good ton heavier than our VAL70 chassis.'

However, despite what some writers have said in the past, the YRT was actually cheaper than the VAL in real terms, for even though it came in at a price of about £3,200, you got more for your money than you did with the VAL14 which cost £1,800 ten years earlier. The trouble is that people forget that this was a time of real inflation, power strikes, coal miners strikes and a government out of touch with the reality of the times. The bus grant situation was a half-hearted attempt by the Tories to address all the problems of the 1968 Transport Act. Labour hadn't got the initial Act right either, but the change of government saw too many worthwhile proposals being scrapped, and a charter being given to private car ownership.

The bus industry was in a mess, granted not as big a mess as would follow de-regulation under Mrs. Thatcher, but a mess none the less; sales of new vehicles plummeted, and the more costly chassis suffered.

In this environment, many firms that had been AEC or Leyland bastions went over to the YRT and a lot of them fitted the new Duple Dominant body. Now you would expect with someone who has a close allegiance to Plaxton to say that the Dominant was a problematic design, but it was; ask anyone who had to rectify the huge problems with the boots on these beasts, for corrosion lead to both expensive re-building and sometimes very short working lives. Plaxton's Panorama Elite was a different story, as too were the offerings from Willowbrook; these were the Executive coaches, and the Spacecar. The Executive was a very boxy design, and the Spacecar had a very apt name; it boasted a hexagonal-shaped front screen, bonded side windows and a complete absence of chrome trim / bright-work. However the Spacecar fitted the grant criteria and in 1975 the National Bus Company purchased two batches of bodies (82 in total we think) and mounted these on either the YRT or Leyland Leopard chassis. Other builders doing well with the YRT were the Portuguese firm Salvador Caetano of Oporto with its Estoril II and Marshall of Cambridge with its Camair service bus.

Bedford had always seen its market as the small, independent operators, but the new grant regime and the need for larger operators to substantially reduce their costs in light of falling traffic receipts meant that bigger outfits were soon knocking on the door at Dunstable. The famous operator Barton increased its stock total of Bedford buses, but it was the purchases of NBC subsidiaries and municipal undertakings that seemed quite remarkable. Scottish Omnibuses Ltd. also opted for the larger chassis, and they ordered a batch of 24, but as a consequence of falling revenue this figure was cut back by four prior to delivery. In 1975 approaching 450 YRTs were sold for the home application, an average of 9 per week, and roughly equivalent to 15% of the total British UK single-deck PSV market. Sales were in a decline though, and whilst Bedford did not experience the same free fall as some manufacturers, they did drop to just under 800 chassis in 1976. The NBC orders continued however, and in 1976 sales of this kind aggregated more than five vehicles every month.

Top Left: *One firm to change from the more expensive Leyland chassis was Cream Line of Tonmawr, who began buying Bedfords when the Davies family bought a pair of YRQs in 1971. After the YRT they also bought a YNT in 1977 before returning to Leyland in 1980.*

Middle Left: *As mentioned previously, the NBC also bought the larger YRT chassis as well as the YRQ, and employed Willowbrook B51-5F bodies. Bearing the appropriate Luton destination blind Eastern Counties 106 (RBD 106M) is a typical example.*

Bottom Left: *The Marshall Camair design, with its excellent visibility is clearly seen on YNO 481L, which was new to Hedingham & District as fleet number L81. The livery was cream and post office red, with gold lettering.*

The only true competitor in the cheap and cheerful under-floor market was Ford's 11-metre R1114 chassis. Sales of the R1114 were only about two-thirds of those on the YRT, but when they turbo-charged their power unit the hoped for sales did not seriously dent the YRT's dominance. Unlike Bedford who mounted their engine amidships, the Ford unit stayed at the front end, and they remained a heavy-nosed affair to drive. I own an R1114, which we christened the 'Shetland Pony', after Mike Berry said that it drove like a rocking horse.

Nevertheless, the YRT's 466 cu. inch power plant was nothing to write home about, and we can honestly say that it was evident from the outset that (as a result) the YRQ was flawed from day one. The initial braking system on the YRT was also suspect, and a massive improvement was affected from the end of 1973 onwards, along with increased gearbox, clutch and steering performance. Quite what happened to the suggestion that Bedford would offer a factory-fitted option on a proprietary-brand diesel power plant (Cummins or Perkins) is unknown. Yet both the YRT and also the YRQ were to benefit from a new 8.2-litre diesel power unit of Bedford manufacture, and the first of these went into test vehicles in 1974. A year later both the YRQ and the YRT would be replaced by YLQ/YMQ and the YMT in 1975.

In concluding our look at the YRQ / YRT, we might just mention the Cascais II that Caetano built in association with Moseley's, a Bedford dealer based in Loughborough. This had the unusual feature of a vertically-mounted Bedford 466 cu. inch diesel engine located at the rear of the chassis. It looked, and sounded like a completely different vehicle to the conventional offerings from Duple, Plaxton and Willowbrook, and to several commentators it also seemed alien as well. Nevertheless, quite a number of independents liked it, but there is no accounting for taste.

Top Right: *This futuristic-looking body fitted to a YRT chassis was considerably ahead of its time. Appropriately named then, the Willowbrook Spacecar, it had a 45-seat body ideal for express coaching duties. It went as a demonstrator to National Travel North East as KWB 471P, but was re-registered KWB 477P in October 1976 when it formerly entered the fleet.*

Middle Right: *By way of contrast, the Willowbrook Executive was a boxy looking body, not dissimilar to the Harrington Legionnaire. This Willowbrook C51F model (used for show and publicity purposes) was new to Perretts, but is seen here with dummy plates as FAY 413L.*

Bottom Right: *You either loved it or you loathed it, at least that was the impression we got about people's perceptions of the new Caetano continental-styled bodywork. Peter Hill writes 'I liked traditional two-colour coach liveries, though the styling of this Portuguese offering did little for me, but it was the start of a new genre. At least they were distinctive, and for what you got included - the price wasn't bad either, so that is probably why many small independent operators went for them!' This 1975 YRT has a C53F body and was new to Turner of Hitchin, better known as Greenway Travel.*

THE SB LIVES ON (NFM & NJM SERIES)

If there is one success story in the annals of British PSV chassis manufacturing, it has to be the humble SB, which was introduced as the Big Bedford at the 1950 Commercial Motor Show. It may never have been a 'big bus' in the truest sense of the word, but it was a major step forward, taking Bedford in to the 33-seat market for the first time. As improvements were developed the seating capacity went up to the 40+ arena, and it stayed as a popular choice for many operators. Who would have thought that those smart Plaxton Panorama III or Duple Dominant bodies were mounted on the same chassis as the bulbous-looking Duple Vega bodies of the early-1950s. Obviously the power plants had changed in the two decades between the SB's introduction and the start of our book, but it was still the same basic chassis.

Above: *This smart and stylish Duple Dominant C41F body on an NJM (SB5) chassis is pictured close to the sea-front at St. Annes before delivery to Warrington's of Irlam in 1974. It was registered CRF 699N. Duple Ltd.*

The original power plant, which appeared in the later OBs, (the 84bhp 6-cylinder petrol engine launched at the 1950 Brussels Motor Show) became known as the SBG; later the SB2. As mentioned earlier, other designations followed:

SBO	Perkins 5.56-litre Diesel (1953-1958)
SB1	Bedford 300 cu. inch Diesel (1957-58)
SBG / SB3	Bedford 300 cu. inch Petrol (1950-86)
SB5	Bedford 330 cu. inch Diesel (1961-86)
SB8	Leyland 350 cu. inch Diesel (1958-61)
SB13	Leyland 370 cu. inch Diesel (1961-68)

Top Left: *New to Great North Eastern Road Services of Darlington, this is one of the original Bedford SB chassis, featuring a Duple Vega body style, built under licence by Brush of Loughborough. However, it is quite appropriate to show this view, as the route on which it was operated has a close connection with the publisher's base at Appleby-in-Westmorland. This was one of the stops on the trans-Pennine 'express' route it followed from Darlington in Co. Durham to Carlisle in Cumberland.*

Middle Left: *The same underneath - almost, this SB (NFM) chassis has the 300 petrol engine and a Panorama III C41F body, and was used by Plaxton as their 1972/3 demonstrator.* Plaxton Ltd.

Bottom Left: *For the 1970s this was an ugly bus - utilitarian PCA 331P may be, but it is a dated and unappealing service bus with Duple Midland body styling. Underneath it has the SB chassis, and a unitary construction body badged as Willowbrook.* Malcolm Knight

The late 1960s saw the abandonment of Leyland diesel engines, so the SB8 (with 350 cu. inch) and the SB13 (with the 370 cu. inch) were no longer available, leaving primarily the SB3 300 cu. inch petrol (NFM) and the SB5 330 cu. inch diesel (NJM) as their contenders in this market. We say primarily, because we have seen late production models fitted with the 300 cu. inch Bedford diesel and also 1970-built chassis with Leyland engines as well. These may well have been fitted retrospectively!

The two standard options were still ideal for most UK operators, as the SB remained primarily a rural bus, a fact testified to by the continued availability of a 7' 6" wide chassis as well as the 8' standard. However, with the opening up of many new motorways in the 1970s, it became increasingly evident that the 330 cu. inch diesel could do with a bit more kick to it. At one stage the 466 was examined as a potential replacement, but this was certainly 'over-egging the pudding'. Yet quite a few operators bemoaned the lack of the SB8 option with its 350 cu. inch Leyland power plant. Brief consideration was also given to go 'under-floor', but the big export market enjoyed by the SB again made this a non-starter.

The answer oddly enough came from Ford's decision to turbocharge its 330 cu. inch diesel engine for use on its mid-weight bus and truck range; which itself had been a reaction to Bedford's introduction of the 466 cu. inch diesel. So in the 1970s an opportunity was taken to examine how the Bedford 330 engine would perform if it too were turbocharged. Turbocharging diesel engines was seen as an ideal means of gaining more power from them without having to undergo substantial research and development costs. The concept would certainly come into its own with the larger coach engines, as we will discuss presently, but it was really the truck market that gave impetus to this move in to the future. Admittedly it was not a quantum leap, but the result was a 6-cylinder 5.4-litre unit producing 107.3bhp as opposed to 98bh. Known as the 5.4/105TD, it was paired alongside the uprated 220D engine and became part of Bedford's "Red Series" engines.

There were other improvements too, including the fitting of the Eaton 5-speed gearbox as standard. Furthermore, in common with the VAS a lot of work was also done on braking systems in the early 1970s in order to bring the chassis up to EEC requirements. Furthermore, the driving position was brought forward to improve close range vision. The other major changes were to the brakes and a new spring loaded parking brake was fitted, as were revised braking systems comparable with those employed on TK and TL truck ranges.

The UK body builders continued to take the NFM/NJM and make it look a 'modern coach', and both Plaxton's Panorama III and the Duple Dominant offerings were impressive. In a way, it made good sense for an operator to keep an SB or two in the fleet, and use the model alongside the larger 11-metre buses. Especially when choosing the same bodywork styling (e.g. the Dominant) for both types, as this gave a family look to any fleet. Of course it was a concept that Duple had done well from with its Bella Vista, Bella Vega and Vega Major in the 1960s, but it worked equally well in the period covered by this book.

Yet it was the export sales that really kept the SB in production for the UK market, and these remained substantial down to the end. For example in 1978, 2,341 NJM (SB5) chassis were sold (an aggregate of over 55 each week), mostly for the export market. In 1970 it dropped to 2,057 of which 1,750 were exported to the Indian sub-continent; Pakistan purchased 1,380, and Bangladesh took 360 in CKD form. By 1981 it had dropped to just under 1,000 as Japanese exports hit the traditional market for the first time. By 1983 just 586 export NJM chassis were sold, plus 15 were petrol engine NFM variants. By the final full year of production just over 500 were sold, but this was still four times the combined total for the Y series chassis sales that year.

Top Right: *Typical of the styling on many of the products made by Marshalls of Cambridge, this NJM chassis has the turbo-charged 330 diesel engine. It was ideal for military transport, and much favoured by armed services in various parts of the world. The body style, known as the Campaigner, usually had 43 to 45 dual-purpose seats. This example was produced for the Royal Kingdom of Brunei.*

Middle Right: *A total of 57,129 SBs were built, making an aggregate of five per day over the years. Chassis for 7' 6" wide bodies were still available in 1987, and Caetano gave two NJMs (SB5s) Aviero bodies. The deal (for Jersey) sadly fell through, so these very late SB models spent some time working at Gatwick Airport, until (on appeal) they were finally supplied to the States of Jersey. After a career with Holiday Tours and Tantiry, D832 CNV was fully refurbished by Martin Perry of Bromyard and put to work on his services in rural Herefordshire. It is seen here when new in 1987. Andrew Webster*

Bottom Right: *A 300 cu. inch petrol engine was the power plant on this demonstrator bodied by the Commonwealth Aircraft Co. of Australia, who were better known as Comair. Their DP43F shown here was marketed as the "workmen's comfort coach", but the same design was also used for school transport as well.*

THE VERSATILE VAS - THE PJK / PFK SERIES

Bedford had long found a niche-market in the low-capacity bus and coach market, as evidenced by its successful W-Series of the 1930s, and the hugely popular OB and OWB models in the 1940s. Its change to the 33-seat SB in the 1950s was a very unpopular move for some operators, especially those in rural communities, where the 7' 6" wide OB had been the life-blood of the public transport system. A rapid introduction of the C4Z or C5Z 29-seat chassis in the late-1950s helped re-build confidence, but the VAS of 1961 cemented the relationships for years to come. Therefore the VAS, or as it was later re-designated the PFK / PJK was another model that would continue in production down towards the end. It would not sell as well as the SB, but it did have sticking power.

22

As the SB's baby sister, it fulfilled a variety of roles, for which either the 300 cu. inch petrol engine (VAS3) or the 330 cu. inch diesel (VAS5) was more than adequate. The former designations had been VAS1 (300 cu. inch diesel) and VAS2 (214 cu. inch petrol), but these were subsequently up-rated as both the original units made you feel as though they were a bit flat. The larger power units performed far better, and these were carried forward into the new generation of designations as the 114bhp PFK (VAS3) and 98bhp PJK (VAS5).

The early 1970s saw even more improvements, but these were basically along the lines as those already discussed in the chapter dealing with the NFM / NJM. The advent of the turbocharged 330D was an improvement too, and when we compared Martin Eltham's 107.3bhp preserved PJK to our 1965 VAS1, the difference was substantial and clearly showed the progressive development of the model.

Nevertheless, the VAS was seen by many as a very dated design; as the protruding engine cowl and entry doors behind the driver prevented the VAS from fulfilling a truly useful role in modern bus and coach operations. Ideally an underfloor version on a short wheelbase chassis was what many operators needed, preferably one giving front entrance. The afore-mentioned short wheelbase Ford R1104 / Duple Dominant C31FT is a good example of this application, albeit hampered by its high chassis height and the number of steps required to climb aboard.

As a consequence of the potential demand, Bedford agreed to allow Tricentrol to shorten a 10-metre YMP chassis to an 8-metre coach, but this was only ever built in small numbers. One wonders how it would have fared had it been formerly adopted as a factory production unit and marketed accordingly. We can only speculate and say that this would have been a significant step forward, and perhaps it was only dismissed due to the falling sales in the bus and coach sector.

Top Left: *Functional capability, the 29-seat VAS was ideal for both PSV and non-PSV applications; including staff transport as seen on OYF 768R, a Duple Dominant purchased by the BBC in 1976.*

Top Right: *With Blackpool Tower, this 1974 Duple Dominant C29F carries a false registration plate DPL 74M as it poses on the beach not far from the Central Pier. It has the 330 cu. inch diesel engine and was a demonstrator for the Blackpool-based coach-builders.*

Middle Right: *Plaxton's competitor in the 'under 30-seat capacity market' was this 29-seat body, fitted to the PJK chassis. Many of its components can be attributed to the standard size Plaxton coaches of the day. New to Moor-Dale Curtis, it was registered TJR 492N.*

Bottom Right: *For 1970, the dealers Moseley launched this version of the VAS/PJK at the Commercial Motor Show. The arrival of the Caetano Sintra was something of a culture shock to many people at the time but in retrospect we think that the 29-seat offering from Moseley / Caetano quite suited the styling. The entry door was a distinct improvement on the doors used by both Duple and Plaxton on the VAS chassis in the 1970s.*

Top Left: *Whereas some builders, such as Anglo and Reeve Burgess experimented with modern styling on the VAS chassis, Strachans could hardly claim this B27F was in the same league. Commonly noted as a VAS3 in fleet books, ERU 403L was actually a PFK as it had the 300 cu. inch petrol engine. New to Bournemouth Transport in 1973 it carried fleet No. M3 and worked mostly on the town centre services.*

Middle Left: *During the 1970s, a series of new ideas were put forward for school bus / welfare bus designs on the PFK/PJK chassis. Vauxhall engineers worked very closely with the firms developing these bodies, including Anglo of Batley, Marshall, Willowbrook, and even Martin Walter who produced this "Dormobile' B31F school bus. It unusually featured entry doors on either side.*

Bottom Left: *A second view of the Eastern Scottish DP17F VAS (FFS 6X) taken at the Forth Bridge car park in 1981. Whereas the view on page 2 shows the road bridge, this one shows the stupendous railway bridge built by the North British Railway. The body on fleet No. 2C-6 had only a 17-seat capacity, as the back end of the body also had a large luggage compartment, and followed a practice employed for many years on the MacBrayne Bedfords employed in the Highlands & Islands of Scotland.*

As the pictures on this page illustrate, the VAS still had a useful non-coaching role to play, and the three examples illustrated show how the 13' 8" wheelbase could be bodied for different service needs. As a school bus it could even exceed the usual 29-seat arrangement, and one model by Anglo could accommodate 42-children. A 1980 Bedford bus brochure proclaimed, 'The VAS caters for applications too big for the CF, too small to justify the operation of one of the larger chassis in the Bedford range. For this type of operation it has all the right features: compact overall width for bodies from 2,280mm (7' 5") to 2,590mm (8' 5"), kerb-to-kerb turning circle of only 15.4m (51') dia., low floor line to give easy entry and exit.' The latter feature being afforded by those 16-inch wheels it had shared with the VAL.

The number of lesser-known builders using the VAS for PSV applications in the 1970s was quite impressive, and includes Anglo Coachbuilders (Batley), Bailey (Bidulph). Hawson (Sunbury-on-Thames), Lex Vehicles (Totton), Pilcher-Greene (Burgess Hill), SMT (Edinburgh), Reeve Burgess (Chesterfield), Smith (Loughborough), Martin Walter (Folkestone), Victory/Wadham Stringer (Hampshire), Walker (Watford), Wright (Ballymena), and possibly Warner of Lincoln. Major builders of course included Duple, Plaxton and Willowbrook, whilst Walter Alexander had some VAS chassis delivered to the works at Glengormley in Northern Ireland.

Of course the VAS had a wide variety of non-PSV applications, and it was sold for use in applications such as ambulances, armoured cars, blood transfusion collection mobiles, mass radiography vehicles, mobile display units, mobile libraries, prison vans, travelling shops, and so on.

Neath 4
B 4287
Cwmavon 2
(B 4286)

Above: *At Pontrhydyfen in the Afan Valley (near Neath) we see NNY 637L, a Bedford YRT / Plaxton Elite II (C53F), which was new to Cream Line Services Ltd., Tonmawr. In addition to being the birth-place of Richard Burton, Pontrhydyfen was famous for the Bont-fawr Aqueduct, which was built about 1825 to supply water for the water wheel and blast furnace at the Oakwood Ironworks. The water-course was four feet wide and three feet deep and flanked by pedestrian paths either side. The 495-foot long bridge no longer carries water, and with the canal having been filled in, it is now only used by pedestrians and cyclists.*

Right: *For the small coach market, the Bedford VAS continued to be a popular choice. By 1979 the VAS had become the Bedford PJK, and it still had an engine that protruded into the passenger saloon, which in turn restricted access to the driver's and front passenger seats. Nevertheless, when fitted with the Duple Dominant body, as seen on DAC 754T, it looks a thoroughly modern vehicle.*

Above: *Although it was never in the same league as the Leyland National or the Bristol LH with ECW bodywork, this combination of a Bedford YRT and Duple bodywork looks every part a modern service bus. The body styling is Duple's service bus version of the Dominant, but bears no resemblance to the coach body of the same name. This example, JKO 63N was new to City of Oxford Motor Services. This firm was founded in 1913 by William Morris, who was also the founder of the Morris Car Company and later became Lord Nuffield. The bus company became Oxford Tramways in 1914 and City of Oxford in 1921.*

Left: *By way of contrast to the rather utilitarian offering for passengers in Oxford, this is the luxury version of the Dominant II. Mounted on a YMT chassis ENS 345T is a C18FT. It was new to Blue & White Coaches in 1978 and offered every conceivable form of executive luxury, including single 'armchair' seats, table, kitchen, TV, conference facilities and so on.*

Above: *Here we see a 1970 Bedford YRQ with Willowbrook DP45F seating in service with Salopia, the well known operator from Shropshire. Although the original owners sold out their interests in the firm, one of its former employees continues the company, which is based in Wem. They were loyal Bedford customers for many years, and several of their vehicles featured in Bedford publicity material*

Right: *For many years, Bedford trucks were the main choice for the British Armed Forces, with examples being supplied to all three main services. Many of the later Bedfords are still in active service, along with a few Bedford buses. Generally those PSV chassis supplied to the Ministry of Defence were given Mulliner, Willowbrook or Marshall bodies. Here we see one of the Royal Navy personnel carriers, which is a Marshall-bodied example. In this 1978 view we see 67 RN 60, a Bedford PFK (a petrol-engined VAS) at an unidentified Royal Naval Air Station.*

Above: *The arrival of the continental body was something of a culture shock to the British market, especially when compared to the rather staid offerings of the British manufacturers. Love them or loathe them, models such as these Caetano bodies certainly changed the face of British coaching. The red and white liveried coach is a Cascais body mounted on a VAM chassis, whilst the blue and white one has an Estoril body on a YRT chassis; both were demonstrators with the Moseley organisation.*

Left: *Here we have another model that helped an 'overseas' manufacturer get well-established in Britain. The Bedford YMT has a C49F body, which was produced in Dublin in a joint venture between Van Hool and the Irish coach-builders McArdle. A connection that ultimately helped springboard Van Hool to its current position of strength in the UK market This vehicle (VAY 310S) was ordered by Shorey Travel of Flitwick in 1978.*

MICRO MAGIC (THE CF SERIES)

The bottom end of the market would prove to be a boom area in the late 1960s and early 1970s, as the mini-bus found its niche. No longer viewed as just a crew-bus or patient transport vehicle, mini-buses went on to achieve great popularity, especially in school transport work. Indeed, the mini-bus of the 1970s was the starting point for many operators running larger fleets today, and into that market Bedford promoted the new CF van-derived mini-bus. Several minibuses would be straight forward conversions of the basic CF, an American-looking panel van that Bedford had introduced to Britain in 1969.

In the previous volume, Mike Berry covered the genesis and development of the CA van, and briefly mentioned the new CF. What he did not cover was the list of 'might have beens' in between, CB and so on, and it is no accident that the designation for the lightweight models jumped from CA to CF. It is not our remit to cover those models in this narrative, as the prototypes that were produced were all light commercials, but had full production been commenced, then we can safely assume that there would have been mini-bus derivatives.

Above: *A CF mini-bus by Williams & Co. of Manchester, who marketed their model as the 'Deansgate' conversion.*

Taking the 1970s as the launch-pad, GM brought out the CF in 1969 with brand-new features and quite a lot of inspiration from GM's panel van styling then being applied in the USA. It was launched on to the UK market in the following different forms: - 14-cwt, 18-cwt, 22-cwt, and 35-cwt.

However it would eventually transform and become a different range that was designated as:-
The CF 230 (2.3-ton) and the CF250 (2.5-ton) vans, or the
CF 230 (2.3-ton) and the CF250 (2.5-ton) chassis-cowls;
all of which had a 106-inch wheelbase.
Then there was the`: -
CF 280 (2.8-ton) and the CF350 (3.5-ton) vans, or the
CF 280 (2.8-ton) and the CF350 (3.5-ton) chassis-cowls,
all of which had a 126-inch wheelbase. And finally there was the
CF350L (3.5-ton) long (140-inch) wheelbase chassis cowl.
Of these the CF230 / CF250 only really gave a work-bus / mini-bus capability, but the CF280 and CF350 each had sufficient headroom in the standard body to permit PSV operation.

Top Left: *It cannot be claimed that the CA was the first of Bedford's micro-buses, as car-derived vans such as the VYC/VXC, BYC/BXC and the PCV had already fulfilled that role in the 1930s or 1940s. However, the CA really did popularise the concept, and for thousands of firms the CA in its various guises from 'Workabus', 'Crewbus' and 'Utilibus' through to the Dormobile, Grovesnor and Kennex minibuses signalled the start of a new era in public or staff transport.*

Middle Left: *The main thrust of the new CF was still seen as a converted panel van for use as a crew bus, or a general purpose vehicle that could equally be used to carry a group of workers, their tools and / or materials. In this form, probably the best-known conversion specialist was Martin Walter of Folkestone. Their long association with Vauxhall, which actually stems back to the post-war E-Type Cresta and Velox, meant their 'Dormobile' name was instantly recognised. For the CF lwb models, they offered a 13-seat or 15-seat conversion on the CF280 and CF350.*

Bottom Left: *The CA had shown a good deal of versatility in the sector of the market dealing with patient transport, and eventually it evolved into more than just a lightweight ambulance. Here we see a 7-seat Walker "Karricar' Welfare ambulance from 1976.*

The two short wheelbase models could easily be adapted by having special bodies fitted to the chassis-cowl version, but these really were too light for serious PSV applications. This was evident in CF250s bodied for use in ambulance applications, for example a fleet of these vehicles used by the County Durham Ambulance Service were laid up at the back of one of Darlington's hospitals in the late-1970s. The reason being that the bodies were too heavy for the chassis, and wheels had been falling off the rear axles whilst the ambulances were in operation!

Engines applied to the CF range were initially carried over from the CA range, namely the Vauxhall 1599cc petrol engine or the Perkins 4.108-litre diesel engine, both of which were offered as options in the 14- and 18-cwt models. However buyers of the 22-, 25- and 35-cwt CF models had the choice of the Vauxhall 1957cc petrol engine or the Perkins 4.154-litre diesel engine. In 1972 the engines were replaced by a GM 2279cc petrol engine or the GM 1998cc diesel engine across the range. Many drivers found these units a bit flat on the larger models, but in the next change 1.8-litre petrol engines were used on the CF230 and the 2.3-litre on the others. Later an improved version of the 2.3 diesel engine was introduced, which then became the 2.3/60D.

There was a choice of gearboxes on each model, on the two smaller models these were the GM 4-speed manual or the GM automatic, whereas the CF 280 had a choice of 4- or 5-speed ZF 'box. The CF350 / CF350L also had the two ZF products on the diesel engine and the GM automatic on the petrol engine. Independent front suspension, rack and pinion steering, dual circuit hydraulic brakes, very long semi-elliptic taper-leaf springs (at the rear) and hydraulic telescopic shock absorbers (front and rear) were among its other features.

The decidedly ugly feature of the CF, to our minds at least, was the tin cowl at the front of the vehicle - Mike Webster of Dormobile described them as 'myopic bugs' when he first saw one at his factory in Kent. Yet as time progressed there were marked body-styling improvements, the most notable of which was described as, 'A re-styled front end including zinc-coated steel for the structural pressings; a non-chip resilient grille of special high-strength hot-moulded plastics.' New, deeper and tougher full-width bumpers with a hard epoxy-powder coating and urethane wrap-rounds. And, finally an underbody and wheel-arch anti-corrosion treatment where bituminised sealer and sound deadener was baked on at 82 degrees centigrade.

For the driver, more comfortable features were provided, notably a Bostrom-designed seat with posture and height adjustment; the whole seat being covered in a simulated Donegal tweed fabric. Better instrumentation and stowage space were provided, but the most noticeable feature was the reduction of in-cab noise. This was achieved by the use of sound deadening materials, re-designed engine and drive line mountings and new rear spring mountings.

The great thing about the CF in chassis cowl form was how easy it was to mount a specialist body upon, thanks to its flat topped, deep box section and unobstructed chassis. The fact that CF chassis were also torsionally strong helped to keep flexing and stress down to a minimum, which was an essential requirement for those body builders working predominantly with glass-reinforced plastic (GRP).

A great many firms bodied the CF chassis-cowl and / or converted the standard panel van for PSV application, some of the notable ones being Howson, Lex, Marshall, Plaxton, Reeve Burgess, Walker, Martin Walter (Dormobile) and Williams (Deansgate) to name but a few.

For us, one of the great things about the CF was the ease of access, if required. For big jobs we could have a body off in under 30 minutes, whereas the entire front end could be taken off in less than a quarter of an hour. Extracting the engine was then a simple task, as it could be withdrawn straight from the front with no obstruction to bar the way.

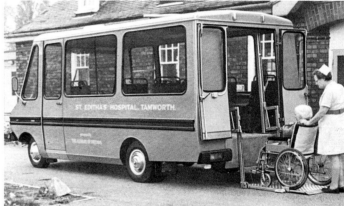

Top Right: *Another firm who offered a variety of conversions to the CA was the Lex Vehicle Engineering Group of Totton in Hampshire. Given that this firm's parent company also had a big hire and leasing operation, it was quite natural that a large number of CFs were supplied. One of the conversions offered by Lex was a 12, 13 or 15-seat personnel carrier on the CF280. Unusually, this offering came with plush seating as standard.*

Middle Right: *Returning to the theme of patient transport, here we see the Reeve Burgess offering on the CF350 chassis cowl. It had a steel-framed body, wheel chair lift and exceptional visibility all the way round.*

Bottom Right: *Experience with the CA and the early CF conversions showed a defined market for the true minibus; to address this need Plaxton offered the 17-seat Mini Supreme on the CF350 chassis cowl, featuring all-metal construction and a laminated top.*

An Old Favourite - The J Series

For the next stage up the PSV spectrum (23-seat and under), Bedford also provided an exciting range of vehicles, the upper capacities being catered for by the coach derivatives of its TJ series. Better known as the J models, this had a range of chassis from 1- to 5-ton, although the most common applications for PSV bodies were the 2-ton and 4-ton chassis, although 3-ton models were not unknown. Collectively they provided a truly cost-effective chassis that could be bodied by a large number of coachbuilders, and many of these were used in what could be termed non-PSV work, such as crew-buses, disabled person's transport, ambulances and the like.

'But why', you may well ask, 'was this 1950s design still being perpetuated at the start of the Glam Rock era?' There are two answers and both are really quite simple; the first is simply that the TJ models sold well all-round the world, and GM's motto seemed to be 'if it isn't broken, don't fix it', the second was the fact that the company had really nothing better with which to replace it.

Above: *Useful and dependable, but not a stylish choice for the 1970s? This J2 (XNY 518H) carries 20-seater Plaxton bodywork and was with Tal-Tax of Llantrisant.* Andrew Webster

John Westfield, who delivered new coaches from Scarborough remarked; 'the 'J', most commonly the J2, remained the real answer to the needs of the 19- to 21- seat UK operator, but bodies like those fitted by Plaxton (based on the Embassy) and Willowbrook really did not look terribly modern. If I am perfectly honest, I have to say that I was never really impressed when I was given the job of delivering these, and I avoided being seen in them whenever I could.'

Equally, we can say that the Duple Midland bus body was something that firmly belonged in the 1950s. In fact the Duple design had really been developed as a derivative of its Almet and Metsec bus bodies that had been introduced for the post-war export market. Of all the bodies applied to the J, we have to say that some of the overseas bodies, such as those made by Comair in Australia looked far more sophisticated than their UK counterparts.

Mechanically, the J type remained the same, and it was a proven formula that was never really supplanted by the TK range intended to replace them. In bus and coach bodying applications, the TK was never really a contender. The position of the engine (behind the cab in the lorry) was in entirely the wrong place for the door position on a front-entry bus.

Realistically, the role of the TJ series would soon be fulfilled by the larger capacity CF models, but at the same time several operators began to choose Ford products. The first of these was the ubiquitous Transit which, after its introduction in 1965, eroded both the CA's and TJ's market place. The up-rated A series, the Transit's big brother, enjoyed some success in the field, but it was the ubiquitous D series that did so much damage to the normal control TJ.

The development of forward control TJ models held out most promise for the 1970s, and it looked good under designs like the Moseley Continental Faro II coach. It was considered as a useful contender in the new urban bus market, of which three sizes of bus were seen as being needed. We have already discussed the VAS and its role in the 29-seat market but there was another proposed contender in the 11-metre range. It would have been built jointly with the body-builders MCW, using components from the TK and KM range and a rear-mounted 466 cu. inch diesel engine.

The Bedford MCW project, and the TJ urban bus all came to nothing as a result of the engines projecting into the body [in the case of the MCW bus in the seating area at the back, and on the TJ into the operating area at the front]. Experience with the VAS operation showed that the entry doors behind the driver necessitated the driver having to twist round to collect fares, and on intensive urban services, this was considered as being impractical and detrimental to good posture. It is very strange that Bedford did not look at an underfloor replacement, especially when the growing demand for such a bus was emerging worldwide as smaller seating capacities were coming into vogue. A plan for a rear-engined version came to naught.

Top Right: *The TJ series was promulgated far longer than one might have expected, and even the earliest designs were still in demand, as seen with this view of two 2-ton chassis with Lomas bodies built for British European Airways at the end of 1969. The vehicles are seen in March 1970 before being sent overseas for use as flight crew buses.*

Middle Right: *A diesel-engined TJ3 fitted with Caetano DP22F bodywork dating from 1972. Little is known about this vehicle, other than it was an export model bound for one of the Balkan states. Can anyone help with information?*

Bottom Right: *By way of contrast, we see a 2-ton TJ chassis with Moseley Continental Faro II bodywork for Jalna of Gresley, who had it as No. 29 in their fleet. Initially delivered to Moseley with a petrol engine, JAY 825N was re-engined with a diesel unit prior to delivery back to the UK by Caetano. The vehicle is pictured here at the Brighton Coach Rally.*

The YLQ/YMQ/YMP Series (10-Metre Chassis)

The 466 cu. inch engine, as significant as it was for Bedford, was really only a stop-gap measure in their quest for greater sales in the bus and coach market. For most operators, the Bedford chassis had been a cheap and cheerful option, and had long been suited to firms who were not doing long-haul jobs day in and day out. For such operators, the choice could really be between AEC and Leyland.

Up to the 1960s there had been a strict demarcation between the express or long-distance operators and the smaller independents; the latter at best doing only a small percentage of their total mileage on long distance runs. When these operators did longer journeys, they tended to be excursion jobs, Blackpool Illumination tours, Skegness Bank Holiday runs and the like. But with the demise of British Railways, thanks to the. 'Beeching Report' and the development of new motorways and better trunk roads as a consequence of the 'Buchannan Report', the whole scene was changing. Those operators who were ready to adapt found that they could pick up substantial levels of new traffic - after all, private car ownership was still a long way off for a lot of people.

Above: *Seen on Scarborough's Valley Road, beneath the imposing Victorian bridge, this early YLQ has just been out-shopped from Plaxton's Seamer Road Works for publicity photographs. It was to enter the fleet of Moor-Dale-Curtis, a dedicated Bedford customer. As a matter of interest, did you know that the large white lighthouse in the background was a World War 1 casualty, after it was hit by a salvo of shells from a German Navy battle-cruiser?* Plaxtons Ltd.

Therefore, Bedford had to face the fact that the 466 was not up to the job that operators were now asking of it, especially given that the motorways were putting more distant holiday resorts, for example the West Country, into the possibility of a 'day-trip' destination. The good old 466 would undoubtedly amble along at 55mph with a full load, but push it past 60mph and.....!

As not all drivers were particularly conservative with their engines on the new, faster roads, more and more instances of 'blown' power units were being reported. In the best case scenario, a lot of blue smoke could be seen trailing from the exhaust pipe. Obviously something more powerful was needed.

The answer was to lay not in the 466, but in America with a Detroit-designed diesel engine that would emerge in this country as the Bedford 500 cu. inch power plant. The Detroit engine had a long and interesting history, and one that is too complex to discuss here, but needless to say, Bedford saw it as an answer to the problems facing their 10- and 11-metre coach range, namely the YRQ and the YRT. However, its introduction into the UK actually had more to do with the quest for better power plants for the new generation of commercial vehicles rather than PSVs.

The first of these was basically a concept model based on a KMR (tipper) chassis and cab, with the Detroit 6V-71 200bhp diesel engine mounted behind the cab. The resulting product, displayed at the 1972 Commercial Motor Show, was a 32-ton gross train weight tractor unit. In the months and years that followed, the Detroit-designed engine appeared in more and more Bedford products, and by a corresponding policy change the 300 cu. inch petrol appeared in fewer and fewer.

It has to be remembered that by this time Bedford were up against a state-owned giant (British Leyland), who had already swallowed great names like Albion, AEC, Daimler and Guy, and who also owned half of Bristol [and effectively controlled all the policy], so the opposition was getting less as time progressed.

Seddon, following its acquisition of Atkinson in the early 1970s had bowed out of the PSV market, Commer-Dodge were somewhere in the wilderness and even the mighty Ford Motor Company were by then out in the periphery. Against this there was a background of severe political and industrial unrest in the country, rising inflation, and the rapid onset of overseas competition. Names like Volvo, DAF and Mercedes all starting to do very nicely, thank you very much.

Yet in the 10-metre coach market, the new YLQ remained the most logical choice, and given their dominance of the sector, Bedford worked hard to ensure that they stayed there. In the designation of the YLQ we have: -

Y   the mid-engine series,
L   the 500 cu. 8.2 litre diesel engine derated to 110 kW power
Q   a GVW of approximately 11,400kg.

Below: *The braking problems with the 16-inch wheels on the Bedford VAL had alienated some operators, as had the 466 cu. inch engine on the YRQ. This loss of customer confidence, coupled with other changes in the bus industry had begun to affect Bedford's sales, but the YLQ began to win back many orders. It was a dependable coach and this 1981 example (CYH 796V) carries a MkII Duple Dominant C45F body for Grey Green. Andrew Webster*

Top Left: *Another view at the British Coach Rally, Brighton, this time showing a Plaxton bodied YLQ. This C36F with tables (TKX 111R) was new to Peter O'Neill of Gillingham trading as The Kings Ferry.*

Middle Left: *The slightly more powerful YMQ chassis seen on this 1978-bodied C45F. Carrying the new Plaxton Supreme IV body, this coach served as a demonstrator for the Scarborough-based firm. Plaxtons Ltd.*

Bottom Left: *A project on which all the Trans-Pennine team were involved - the refurbishment of OUF 669W for Vauxhall Heritage. Originally new to Bywaters of Rochdale, the vehicle was re-registered by Shamrock & Rambler. It was extensively refurbished between January and June 2002 and painted in a two-tone green livery. It is pictured here at Appleby Grammar School in February 2002.*

For a while the derated power unit was considered to be more than adequate, but as time progressed, experiments with the same power unit operating at 119kW power showed significant improvements. Then when it was turbocharged to produce 130kW there was a revolutionary change. This was therefore the advent of the YMQ, a designation that meant Y = mid-engine series, M = 8.2 litre 500 cu. inch diesel. In due course a turbocharged version of this engine was fitted with the majority rated to 130 kW, but bigger power outputs were possible.

Paul Robinson from Carlisle said 'I recall taking a 10-metre chassis with a Duple Dominant II body empty to Birmingham, which was fitted with the 500 cu. inch diesel turbo charged to 153 kW power (effectively a YNQ) and a speedometer that was not working. Approaching Knutsford I overtook a lightly loaded Volvo being driven by a Scottish operator of my acquaintance, a mile or so further on I pulled into the service area for my one-penny meal, and was just sitting down when the Volvo driver came in. He walked over to me and smiled sweetly saying, "I never knew you could get 90mph out of a Bedford." I watched my step all the way to Selly Oak after that!''

We are not sure if YNQ was an official designation or not, as we have found no literature to support this, but there is one well-known example that can be seen on the rally circuit in the form of Vauxhall Heritage Services' mobile display unit. When this vehicle was being restored in 2002, we decided that one or two parts were beyond refurbishment and required replacement. When we came to order these, we noticed that the vehicle's serial number actually began with the letters YNQ.

The final variant was the YMP, which was effectively a YMQ with either a 160bhp or a 175bhp turbocharged diesel version of the 500 cu. inch diesel. The 160bhp unit being what was a naturally-aspirated engine, and the 175bhp being the 'low-blow'. By combining the new turbocharged engines with higher-geared rear axles, the coaches travelled at almost precisely the same speed, and could easily do 70mph without stressing either the engine or the passengers; thereby prolonging both the life and reliability of the vehicle into the bargain!

THE YMT SERIES (11-METRE CHASSIS)

We have mentioned in the previous chapter the need for a more powerful unit for the larger Bedford coach chassis, and if this was desirable for a 10-metre chassis it was desperately needed for an 11-metre one. By the mid-1970s British Leyland had really moved their coach chassis range to the top flight, and no longer satisfied with 9.5-litre engines, they had given the 11-metre AEC Reliance and Leyland Leopard chassis 11- or 12-litre diesel engines.

What is more, with the growing weight of the YRT and associated bodies, the difference between a Bedford and a Leyland Group vehicle was nowhere as significant as it had been in the days when AEC and Leylands were known as the heavyweights, and the SB seen as a lightweight.

Above: *Elegance in the valleys, this 1977 Plaxton Supreme C53F body is fitted to a YMT chassis for Hills of Tredegar.*

The introduction of the 500 cu. inch power unit could never be seen as a serious competition to the Reliance or the Leopard, but they did provide a compromise option. The real choice for the operator was one of cheap and cheerful (and slightly improved) or long-term rugged dependability. As both options were now capable of carrying identical bodywork, especially the Plaxton or Duple offerings, the obvious criterion was the initial purchase price of the chassis. In other words, could the difference between the two acquisition costs be recouped by the undoubtedly greater longevity of the Leyland product? Obviously a great many operators believed that it could and Bedford sales declined!

Top Left: *Carrying Plaxton Supreme IV C53F bodywork, DWK 410T was new to Smiths Coaches (Shenington) Ltd in 1978. This fleet was more usually identified by the name Smiths of Tysoe, but DWK 410T also carries the name Globus Gateway on the sides of this red and white liveried coach.*

Middle Left: *New to the George Ewer Group and allocated to the fleet of Grey-Green Coaches Ltd., TYE 723S was a Duple Dominant MkII C49F fitted with the optional front roof destination box. This moulding could either carry a roller destination blind, a blind and route number combination or simply an illuminated panel to display the operator's name.*

Bottom Left: *Another YMT / Duple Dominant II combination is seen here with BNO 695T, which was an ideal bus for both stage carriage and express work. It entered the fleet of Eastern National as a DP53F in 1978 as fleet number 1209 and was fitted with twin-leaf (grant-specification) front doors.*

Yet for many operators, especially the ones with tighter cash-flow, the answer was simply to remain with Bedford, the richer more pragmatic ones would always buy the best, so the real battle lay in the middle ground and with big fleets who were always looking at ways of saving money. In larger fleets, the issue of reliability was not always of primary consideration as a spare vehicle could usually be found in case of a service failure, but for a smaller operator, the consequences of his front-line coach going down could be dire. It was in this battle for hearts and minds that Leyland were slowly edging in front.

As a consequence the need for a better power unit was, like a Plaxton product of the day, paramount! The higher-rated 157bhp 500 cu. inch unit may not have been the ideal answer, but it was one answer. The reason for having a higher rating than that employed on the Bedford truck range was fairly obvious, but one that nevertheless requires stating again. With the higher rated, but rpm governed form used in the PSV application, the 500 cu. inch engine was still naturally faster revving than the big capacity units used by AEC and Leyland. But equally they did not need to rev as high as those used in the Bedford truck range. The reason for this being that coach applications required a higher road speed than commercial vehicles, and at the same time suffered far less stress. Therefore the engines as applied to the PSV chassis tended to be far quieter and much less tiresome for passengers.

We have already talked about turbocharging the Bedford diesels in earlier chapters, but its importance was more noticeable in the 11-metre 49- to 53-seat coach range. These became known as the "Blue Series" engines and came in two ratings, namely the 8.2/130TD, which produced 130.1bhp 2,500rpm and the 8.2/175TD, which produced either 171.2bhp or 173.1bhp at 2,500rpm; this compared favourably with the naturally aspirated engines 150.5bhp 2,500rpm.Even so, there was still a move towards more power, and Bedford would eventually go into the 200+ bhp range with a new engine for the YNT as they continually strived to catch the bigger end of the market..

Whilst Bedford was long-established in the coaching sector, their performance in the stage carriage side of the business had been considerably lacking. Oh true, they had done quite well as a rural service bus, but the big fleet orders bypassed them. It had of course dabbled in the market place with both the YRQ and the YRT, especially those bodied with the service bus variant of the Duple Dominant, but many operators felt that the 466 cu. engine was far from ideal for the stop-start and crawl life of a municipal operation.

With the flop of Britain's first pioneering integral bus, the Seddon Pennine RU (which incidentally Bedford had a chance to take over), the single-deck service bus market came to be dominated by the Workington-built Leyland National. On average one brand-new National entered service every 12 hours during 1973, so it will be seen that a phenomenal market existed. To a lesser extent Bristol enjoyed a reasonable level of growth, yet Bedford believed that it could also do well in what was already a crowded sector. Considerable attention was paid to this area of business, but for whatever reason, the firm seems to have settled back into its concentration on the coaching market.

However, that did not stop extensive efforts to capture some of the NBC subsidiaries' business, and the result was a number of dual-purpose and grant specification YMTs entering service. The real problem was the limitations of the 11-metre chassis, as many long-distance operators were now seeking 12-metre chassis, which had been legal since 1968. The extra capacity was seen as essential for operators facing an already difficult climate, but the only offering from Bedford came from the Dunstable-based firm of Tricentrol.

Tricentrol, in addition to offering a shortened (8-metre) form of the YMQ, also offered a 12-metre extension on the YMT. Whilst these conversions were mentioned in Bedford brochures from the early 1980s, very few can have been made, and already the YMT's days were numbered. Nevertheless, as the 1970s drew to an end, the bulk of the Y-series sales were for YMT models, rather than the YMQ.

Top Right: *A 1978-built YMT chassis fitted with the distinctive Unicar GT80 C53F bodywork. It carries a Leeds registration plate, and was new to Hargreaves Eurover Ltd. of Morley. This firm had been a long-term Bedford customer, and had purchased a large number of SB models in the 1960s.*

Middle Right: *Another view of the body style carried on the YMT by Van Hool/McArdle (see page 28). When this styling is compared with that shown on page 39 of* Bedford Buses of the 1930s & '40s, *it shows just how far Continental designs had progressed. New to Shorey Travel of Flitwick, VAY 310S carried the name* Lady Diana.

Bottom Right: *Now this view of a YMT may confuse some who are not very familiar with one of Bedford's body-builders, namely Lex Vehicles of Totton, Hampshire. This model, named the Maxeta, was designed as a personnel transport, offering dual-purpose seating in the 49- to 53- seat capacity. It was envisaged that it would be ideal for military, police and works' bus applications.*

A New Generation?

At the start of the 1970s, the Bedford directors were keen for the company to have a product for every sector of the bus market, including a new Heavy Duty bus and a double-decker. The only apparent exception being a Midi-bus, but this was due to the fact that very high-level and secretive talks were being held with Seddon about the possible acquisition of their bus business following the Oldham firm's purchase of Atkinson. At the time it was said that Bedford had no interest in the midi-bus market, but events soon showed that to be untrue.

If you were to read page 27 of the booklet *Bedford Buses & Coaches Since 1931*, which this series of books is intended to supplement and replace, you will see it says: 'As this is being written [1979], Bedford is about to start production of another bold new design in the bus / coach field. This is the JJL midi-bus, originally shown in prototype form at the 1976 Commercial Motor Show in London. For Bedford particularly, and for the bus / chassis design generally, the JJL is a novel and thoroughly practical concept for small / medium passenger vehicles.'

Above: *Three JJLs (9008-9/11) entered the municipal fleet at Maidstone, following their hire of 9011 in the Spring of 1981, when 9011 (seen above as HKX 553V) was damaged in an accident, 9010 was purchased in its place. On its repair 9011 was sold to Rowland's of St. Leonard's, but later was acquired by AWD who proposed to re-introduce the JJL in view of a re-emerging demand, but once again nothing ever came of the plan!* Roadmaster

Bedford publicity material of the time said of the JJL; 'It is of semi-integral chassis / body design. The 330 cu. inch diesel engine is mounted transversely at the rear of the body, and it drives it through a fully automatic gearbox.' In reality the JJL was the company's alternative to the Seddon Midi-bus, and was jointly developed with Marshall of Cambridge who had already designed a 7' 6" wide commuter bus body called the BB80 based on a Leyland chassis.

On this subject Leo Taylor recalls, 'Our MD, Bob Price, had always been a bit miffed that he couldn't tell when he saw a Bedford coach, for once the bodies were on them, they could be any make; mind you we engineers had no problem identifying our products, as we could always tell a 466 engine by the blue smoke!'

He continues; 'The MD's problems were compounded by the fact that Plaxton's were giving us grief about fitting our badge and lettering, as their Castle badge took pride of place. As he wanted a bus that everyone could tell was a Bedford, he asked our Styling Department to take Marshalls bland offering and come up with some ideas; I had to prepare the mechanical specifications on what had to be a low cost project. Styling re-designed the body, but it got heavier and longer and the costs went up. Marshalls were given an order to build four prototypes and in 1976 the styling model was shown at Earls Court. It was the star of the show, but all was not well. Cracks were beginning to develop in the working relationship, our systems and methods were incompatible, costs were rising and potential volumes were dropping.

After the show, work was suspended for six months. Parts were sent to Cambridge for fitting, but they had no skilled fitters, their men couldn't recognise them, and they had no stores system. Parts were just scattered across the floor, so we had to send fitters, engineers and a storeman to sort things out, and this was not part of the plan.

When the prototypes were delivered, we found detail differences in what should have been identical vehicles. Then, when testing began in 1978 and we asked Marshalls for spare parts, they did not always fit as the structures were individually built. Then there was acrimony over the way we were testing it, they had built it to run on roads, and we were testing on the rough track at our Millbrook Testing Ground (as Bedford did with all new products), but they did not agree. When Bedford Quality Control people went to Cambridge to audit the production facilities, they found what we engineers had been saying all along, there were none! There were no build records, no gauges, no torque wrenches, no proper equipment for filling and bleeding out brake equipment, and no rollers to check that the brakes actually worked and were balanced. The list was endless.

A quality plan was not agreed and Bedford sought to withdraw from the project, which in my opinion was ill-founded from the start. The whole affair cost the Bedford Engineering budget dearly, but if we had simply sold Marshalls the units they had wanted in the first place, both companies could have made a bit.'

One of the reasons for the poor sales potential of the JJL can be put down to the fact that the 'dial-a-ride' and 'park-and-ride' schemes promoted by the Government in the early 1970s went out of favour, and in the mid-1970s it was estimated that sales of these types of bus would amount to no more than 150 to 200 per annum.

Top Right: *Bedford's manufacturing systems and records were impeccable, they had to be. All parts sources were traceable, and in case of future problems (service, recalls, litigation) an audit trail was easily achieved.*

Middle & Bottom Right: *The four prototype JJLs were sold by Marshalls in 1981, but they were not badged as Bedford products. They were used in Brighton on the Station to Churchill Square Shuttle, and proved quite adequate for the job, as seen here with EKX 646T (centre) and EKX 645T (lower).* Roadmaster Collection

LAST ENDEAVOURS - THE YNT SERIES (11-METRE CHASSIS)

Although the YMT had pretended to be in the 'big league' its true role in life was as a reasonable middleweight, and it was therefore ideally suited as a 48- to 49-seat model. But, by reason of the aforementioned power problems, it still did not perform in all the ways that were expected of an 11-metre coach for the late-1970s.

Over the latter years of the decade, Bedford engines started to get a 'reputation' for serious failures. In my experience, these failures were usually modest affairs to start with, and mostly stemmed from oil or water pump failures. However, as drivers tended to put more pressure on their charges, the problems did not end there and more serious faults developed. A consequence of the water pump problem could be the complete failure of the fan, and if this broke away it caused serious danger to the radiator. The matter became so serious as to involve the operators' trade associations. As a result, rapid 'solutions' were effected, but some were too hasty and the problems continued, and Vauxhall's reputation slipped even more!

Above: *Owned from new by David Platt of Huddersfield Road, Lees, near Oldham, this Bedford YNT carries a Plaxton Paramount III 3200 body. It was new in 1987 as E908 EAY but was later re-registered MIL 6972.* Andrew Webster

Another problem was the fact that operators were demanding higher specifications on their coach bodies, and as the extras went on, so did the weight. Before long the combined result of these factors allowed Leyland products to finally edge ahead of Bedford in the coach market, and in 1980 the YMT dropped to third place in the single deck sales table behind the Leopard (1st place) and the National (2nd). More worryingly, this was also a time when many disaffected Bedford operators began switching to newcomers like DAF, MAN or Volvo!

Bedford's solution was a new model designation with an engine producing 200+ bhp. Hence, in 1981, the YNT was born. This chassis was fitted with the 8.25/205TD at 2,500rpm, even so a larger capacity engine would have improved matters considerably.

Top Right: *Here we see Buckby's of Rothwell EBD 188X, a Bedford YNT with a 1982 Plaxton Supreme V body. This firm operated many scenic European excursion tours, and this one is taking the road over the Sustenpass in the Bernese Oberland's. The road runs from Innertkirchen, near Meiringen, and at this point has reached an elevation of 7,236 feet (2224m) on its journey to Wassen; who says Bedfords can't climb hills?* Malcolm Knight

Middle Right: *By way of contrast, for service and school work, Buckby's had a Duple Dominant-bodied YNT. Although only an 11-metre bus, it has a B65F capacity due to using a 3+2 seating arrangement. Seen here on a layover between journeys to Stamford, OBX 453Y is still operated by this firm from Rothwell, Northamptonshire.* Malcolm Knight

Bottom Right: *This YNT (D822 ERU) features a Duple 320 body. It is seen here in the livery of Scraggs Coaches, Bucknall, Staffs but had just been sold at the Manchester Auctions.* Andrew Webster

From the outset the YNT had the Turner M6 gearbox, but it could be both noisy and troublesome, so until the problems were rectified some models were given a ZF 'box instead. One good thing was the ability to have a direct top gear instead of an overdrive thanks to modifications on the rear axle. Although this axle was basically that used on the KM truck, the original spiral-bevel gear was replaced by a new hypoid gear. As a matter of record, we should perhaps mention that more or less simultaneous with this change, the lighter chassis also benefited from a new medium hypoid axle as well.

The new power unit, which was well received from the outset, would have also benefited older YMT models. However, it carried with it a problem that made its application in anything other than a YNT difficult; basically it was too big. It stood just over an inch higher than the earlier engine, and to accommodate it in the chassis, it was mounted about half an inch (12.7mm) lower. To fit it into a YMT wasn't an impossibility, but it was an awful job and frankly not worth the bother. Second-hand prices of YMTs were not brilliant.

Although the YNT did quite a lot to restore Bedford's image, and it was their top of the range model, they did not sell well; production figures barely exceeded an average of three YNTs every week. The diminishing market, foreign competition, a vigorous campaign by Leyland and a whole other host of factors continued to play a part in the downfall of both this model and the Marque as a whole.

Oddly, despite the reservations that both Bedford and the body builders had expressed about over-specification of bodies on Bedford chassis, an 'approved' 12-metre YNT conversion was offered. This appeared in the 1982 sales brochure, and was again an offering from Tricentrol of Dunstable. This company's base was within a few minutes drive of the Bedford bus and truck plant in the town, and ideally located for the conversion work. However, this could not be taken as a serious attempt on the 12-metre market, and we wonder just how many 'stretched' YNTs were produced as no record seems to have survived!

Top Left: *In producing any book on Bedford, we have to bear in mind that the Marque was not just limited to British operators, indeed the Bedford name sold far and wide and even down to the end, exports accounted for a substantial portion of the company's business turnover. Obviously some countries were very fond of the Dunstable-made buses, and small island states like Malta are still running Luton-built O-Types (though not for much longer). New Zealand was another country that had a partiality to Bedford models, and here we see YY 9412 in service with De-luxe Travel of Blenheim, New Zealand. It was bought at auction ex-K Line and was one of five Plaxtons with a NZ front owned by this company. In total Premier had five YNTs, but all were re-powered with 6BG1TI Isuzu engines and gearboxes.*

Bottom Left: *Typical of Bedford instrument panels on a variety of models over the years, here we see the driving position on the YNT shown above.* Both Gary Smith, De-luxe Travel

As with the YMT, the principle bodybuilders were Duple and from them came the attractive Laser body. This was primarily for coaching applications, but it also came with a choice of dual-purpose or service bus seating. For example, here in the North one of the independent operators in Co. Durham, the Park Motor Co. of Langley Park, found the YNT/Laser combination ideal for its services in and out of Durham City. The Plaxton offering tended to be the Supreme V, and of course the continental builders all had their products as well.

An interesting newcomer was Wrights, the Ballymena-based firm who had received so much support from the Northern Ireland Development Corporation. With a bit of added assistance from Vauxhall as well, they went on to produce the sparkling Contour body. This was a marked contrast to the rather ugly bodies produced by this firm at first, all of which looked more like prison buses than something a self-respecting operator would employ.

Sadly, for Bedford the sales remained disappointing, and were far from the heady days of the Big Bedford and the Duple Vega body! Yet the partial deregulation that came about due to the 1980s Transport Act saw some increase in demand, although this was mainly in the long distance coach market sales, and thus benefited Leyland and Volvo more than it did Bedford and the YNT.

However, the YNT continued to enjoy its 'big coach' role with many small operators, mainly on the grounds of cost. Even so it is interesting to note that it was still chosen by some of the bigger operators, like Barton for example. This famous operator had bought many Bedford chassis over the years (186 between 1964 and 1986 to be precise), and mixed these in and amongst its fleet of AEC and Leyland heavyweights.

Barton bought several batches of YRT and YMT chassis, but fleet numbers 593-602 (PTV 593-602X) were its only YNTs, all of which were fitted with Plaxton C53F bodies. This was a good order given the economic climate of the time, but it was nowhere near the excellent business obtained from the Chilwell firm when it bought no less than 35 YRTs in one go; these being fleet numbers 1337-1372 (YVO 267-302M) with Duple Dominant C53F bodies.

A FINAL VENTURE - THE YNV (12-METRE CHASSIS)

In the final analysis, the YNV came far too late for Bedford, and although hindsight is a wonderful thing, one has to wonder if the company should have just concentrated its efforts in the 8- to 10-metre lightweight range, and given improved power to these chassis (and thereby supported its traditional market) instead of continually striving to fight the Leyland group and the growing foreign competition.

The YNV was therefore probably doomed from the outset, but its launch in the Autumn of 1984, under the name Venturer was a valiant 'final attempt'. Unique in being not only the last Bedford PSV model, but also the first to carry a name rather than a set of designation letters, the Venturer was suitable for 12-mtre bodywork. It also came in at the modest chassis price of just over £24,000.

Another plus point was the chassis weight of 4.47 tonnes, which with a typical body would rise to 12.5 tonnes GVW. With a simulated full passenger and luggage weight the result was about 14.5 tonnes, for which the 8.2/205TD engine was quite appropriate. It was when the weight crept up to 16.25-tones (permitted on optional tyres) that the problem of power again reared its ugly head.

Above: *One of the very few Bedford YNVs with Caetano Algarve I bodywork, D508 WNV is seen prior to its delivery to Ronsway of Hemel Hempstead, outside what was the Caetano's UK headquarters in Tyne Road, Northampton.* Andrew Webster

This made many operators suspicious, or at best reserved, but the truth of the matter is that the intention had been to have a choice of three engines, namely; the 8.2/205TD, the GM-Isuzu 250bhp 6-cylinder, and the Cummins 10-litre LT10. The Isuzu was discounted on the basis that high development costs could not be recouped within a reasonable period due to the low sales forecast of the YNV; but as this engine was fitted in Bedford models in Australia, New Zealand and India, one wonders what these high costs were.

It was then said that the Cummins unit would have 'resulted in a loss of profit', but one Bedford engineer we spoke to said, 'we were fitting these engines as an option in the TM truck range, so there was no reason why we couldn't have done the same in the bus; it was just as though someone up high wanted the project to fail.' The option of a 250bhp Cummins would have appealed to many operators, especially those who were buying Volvos, so this seems to have been an especially short-sighted policy by the firm.

Top Left: *Hardly the best in quality, this picture from Martin Eltham shows the unique sight of Bedford's last big push in the promotion of its PSV range. Taken at the 1985 coach show it shows the YNV in chassis form, flanked by a Duple Laser for Youngs of Cambridge and a Plaxton Paramount 3200 for Excelsior Holidays of Bournemouth.*

Middle Left: *The YNV chassis, was at a price that made it a favourable competitor against the Volvo chassis that were making such major in-roads in to Bedford's traditional market. The air suspension gave it good riding qualities, although many operators were still suspicious over its engine. It is worth mentioning that, in a later form (with the Cummins engine) the natural successor of the YNV was a product not from Bedford but Dennis!*

Bottom Left: *With a Plaxton Paramount 3200 body, D569 RKW is seen in York Pullman liver, but was new to N&R Coaches of Elsecar near Barnsley.* Andrew Webster

The Venturer was a failure due to external sources, the first of which was the feelings of distrust that many operators had about the 8.25-litre engine. Then there was the 'global market' policy being expounded by GM, whereby models were being seen as unviable if they could not be sold simultaneously in several countries. The second was a general downturn in the UK motor vehicle manufacturing industry, which in itself was part of a greater meltdown of British manufacturing thanks to the iconic policies of a Grantham grocer's daughter. That same 'Iron Lady' all but decimated the power of the trade union movement, thereby weakening 'worker's resistance' to management 'cut-back' plans.

It was a terrible era in which the powers of people working in traditional industries (and by implication their leisure pursuits) diminished. Just ask anyone from a steel-making or coal mining community if you need proof. Whereas 'Yuppie power' grew and grew; but ask any coach operator how much 'Yuppies' contributed to their business in the mid-1980s and do not expect to have a polite reply. Add to it de-regulation and all the attendant nightmares, tatty vehicles and bus wars that it brought about, and it is little wonder that YNV sales were as low as 124 in 1984, 36 in 1985, and just three in 1986.

Actually the figures for 1984/5 are somewhat artificial, given that the YNV was only launched in October 1984, this would suggest that a huge number were sold in the last quarter of that year. In fact it was not the case, as a fair percentage of these were made for stock, and we understand two x 100 order batches were sanctioned for building. The first batch would have spanned 1984-5, the second 1985! However it is believed that just one single batch was built in one go, as it was thought that this would reduce manufacturing costs. One interesting fact, is that on Friday 29th March 1985, 63 YNT chassis were shown as 'un-allocated stock'. Six months later the figure was down to just five.

Ironically, despite the poor sales, the YNV, with its superb air-suspension, was a lovely coach to drive. What a shame that it did not have the full, unqualified support from those who really ought to have given it!

END OF AN ERA

One supposes that in this chapter we should set out reasons, give answers or explanations, tell horror stories, but we won't. It is perhaps kinder to say that with UK demand falling, the end was inevitable. Yet the combined total of all coaches sold in 1981 (1,500), was 1,100 units lower than it had been two years previously. Bedford's PSV chassis sales were abysmally poor, and including export orders the decline can be charted as:-

1978	4,295	1982	534
1979	3,523	1983	1,010
1980	1,743	1984	708
1981	761	1985	431

The fact that the export market had buoyed up home sales can be well illustrated in 1983, when 60% of the production had been exported SBs. Yet even the exports were in the doldrums, and new models were earnestly needed, and thus came about the under-floor BOV models. In this designation the O means open, though in reality the choice of engine would have been the 8.2/160 or 8.2/175TD, making it a BMV, or the 8.2/205TD making it a BNV. The 160bhp unit had either the Allison MT643 automatic gearbox or the ZF65/65 six-speed 'box, whilst the other two models just had the ZF.

Above: *Listed as a VAS5, this would be more correctly described as a PJK, but nevertheless was still in production nearly a quarter of a century after its introduction. This particular chassis has a Plaxton Supreme IV C29F body and was new to Glynglen Ltd. (t/as Tri-Star Coachline) of North Finchley, London, in 1985.*

The BOV was derived from the TM truck range, and came with a TM truck front, although the front axle was set back to allow a front-entrance bus. Wrights even bodied an attractive prototype, and about 50 chassis were built. Even so it did not catch on, and the export market slipped further and further away. With no real high volume sales to stimulate new investment, GM simply got tired with the bus and coach operation, and it seems that in general Bedford did nothing to light anyone's fire in the corporate headquarters!

The GM goal was for world models, and Bedford simply did not fit the ideology any more. So the writing was on the wall, and after half a century it was with a feeling of betrayal that the remaining staff went over to the AWD operation. There things just got worse and it was no better when Bedford became part of Marshall SPV either. It all ended ignominiously in 1999 when Bedford production finally ceased, but perhaps others better placed than us should write the reasons behind this sad story!

TRUCK-DERIVED BUSES

From the development of the very first British-built Chevrolet models, Bedford buses had a close affinity with their truck counterparts. Variations of the truck chassis for PSV application were made, and subsequently identified by the addition of the letter 'B' to the chassis designation e.g. OB, SB and so on. It was really only with the development of the new TK range in the 1960s that a real demarcation between the truck and bus ranges arose. As stated earlier, the engine position on the TK did not readily lend itself to PSV applications. There was a commonality of parts however, and the family genre continued.

Nevertheless the TK (and its derivatives) did not remain aloof from the privilege of passenger-carrying, and some really interesting vehicles came about as a result. Few of these were what you would really call PSVs, but there were quite a number of crew bus applications, where box-like cabins were carried on the chassis behind a self-enclosed cab. This was not a problem where the driver did not need to have person-to-person contact with the passengers. Of course, such an arrangement would not have met Construction & Use Regulations in the UK, and the high steps to the cabin floor were another drawback - ask anyone who had to climb up into a British Railways crew-bus after a hard day's slog in the permanent way gang.

Above: *The 'special application' buses that were produced on Bedford chassis were quite numerous. It was a long held practice to use Bedford tractor units to tow bus bodies, especially as people-movers on airports both at home and abroad. This TK ballast tractor and bus was produced for British Overseas Airways Corporation (BOAC) by Thomas Harrington of Hove.*

The other option for passenger carrying (or more correctly people-moving) was the use of a trailer unit with a tractor unit as the prime-mover. This could take two forms, the first of which was the ballast or drawbar tractor, the other being an articulated tractor. In the latter form, it could be either a tractor fitted with a Scammell-type (mechanical horse) coupling, or a fifth-wheel coupling.

Such tractor and semi-trailer applications had been commonly used as people-movers from the days of the O-Type tractor fitted with a Scammell coupling (OSS). These had been used for a variety of applications from airport buses to staff buses, usually drawing large capacity 'bus' trailers manufactured by Dyson or BTC. A good example of these people-movers was the large fleet of OSS-Dyson units operated by the John Sommers Steel Works at Shotton. However, these were not licensed for operating stage carriage or private hire services, and had therefore a limited application. Even so, the concept continued and TA-, TD-, and S- types all found such employment before the advent of the TK.

Top Right: *The three sets of windscreen wipers and distinctive front end may give away the fact that this was based on the Bedford TM truck chassis. Designated the BOV, about 50 of these chassis were built. This example for Nigeria was bodied by Robert Wright & Son in Ballymena and could carry 41 seated passengers and 59 standees.* Wrightbus

Middle Right: *Built by Victory Coachbuilders of Portsmouth (part of the Wadham Stringer group), this Bedford TM 1120 4x4 chassis makes an unusually high floor bus. What is more remarkable is the fact that it was designed to carry 32 passengers, although this might be explained by the fact that it was intended for the African market.*

Bottom Right: *One of the lesser-known builders on Bedford chassis was Anglo of Batley, who may be better known for their work on fire appliances. This was the TT On-Off Highway Bus, which was also based on the TM 1120 4x4 chassis cab. It had a steel-framed body with aluminium panelling and seated 25-passengers.*

Whilst Bedford trucks of all kinds could be used for 'passenger-carrying specials', it was primarily the TK model that found itself being used in this regard. For rigid chassis and drawbar tractor application the TK came in the following ranges:- Four-wheel TK570, TK750, TK860, TK1000, TK1260, TK1470 and TK1630. Six wheel, TK860, TK1000 and TK1260. For these two ranges there was a wide choice of engine ranges (according to model specification), including the 214 cu. inch 86hp petrol and the 220 cu. inch 65bhp; for those who preferred diesel there was the 330 cu. inch 98bhp, the 500 cu. inch 126bhp and the 500 cu. inch 151bhp.

As a tractor unit the choice was limited to the TK1630, TK1930 and TK1930 low-load, with a choice of either the 330 cu. inch 98bhp or the 500 cu. inch 126bhp diesel.

The GVW of the TK series ranged from 5.6-ton to 19-ton, so there was plenty of choice for truck-based 'bus' applications, but for those who wanted rugged, go-anywhere capability, the Bedford M4x4 was the answer. In this range the needs of the military, all-terrain users (for example oil drilling or utility customers) were amply catered for, although the real market place was in export sales to countries with unmade roads. The M1120 came in two basic models, offering a choice of twin or single wheels on the rear axle. It had a 138-inch wheelbase and a 9.5-ton GVW. It came with an engine choice of either the 300 cu.inch 114bhp petrol or the 330 cu.inch 98bhp diesel, although you could have the 500 cu. inch 126bhp to special order.

Body builders on these truck chassis tended to be more limited than the coach / bus builders, but they nevertheless included well-known names like Anglo Coachbuilders, Hawson-Garner, Lex Vehicles, Marshall, Reeve Burgess, G. C. Smith, Victory, Wadham-Stringer and Willowbrook. The vast majority went overseas and two to three decades later some are still at work, especially in African countries where they remain a testament to the skills of both their builders and the operators who keep them in daily service.

TESTING TIMES

One of the facets about any product range, are the untold stories that went on behind the scenes, the every-day occurrences that seemed so ordinary at the time, but now form part of an interesting social and mechanical history. To this end, we asked a former Vauxhall / Bedford engineer, Barry Harvey of Ampthill, about his recollections of working with the product range. He writes,

'At an early stage in the proceedings, we would send off the coach chassis prototypes to various body-builders including Duple, Plaxton, Metro Cammell Weymans and so on, where they would be fitted with bodies, these often being to a new design as well. It was an exciting drive to take a chassis all the way to Blackpool, Scarborough or the Midlands as we had an open chassis-cowl with a very low centre of gravity. Coupled to a high power-to-weight ratio, the chassis would handle like a sports car, albeit a rather large one. The problem was you sat on a crude wooden seat with no cushion or seat belt. If you hit a kerb for instance, you could be thrown off; all illegal these days of course.

Above: *A 1971 publicity picture featuring a YRQ with a Willowbrook DP45F body. This vehicle was new to Vauxhall as a demonstrator, and is seen with one of the most famous Bedford buses of all times in the background; namely TM 9347 the first Bedford WHB bus, which was fitted with a Waveney body. It was new to John Woodham of Melchbourne in 1931.*

When they came back to Bedfordshire, the bodies were fully trimmed and when test work commenced were loaded with canvas bags full of sand, each one about 56lbs. three to a seat. The seats were protected with vinyl covers made by our Trim Shop and the bags were strapped in place, essential as some of the test work, particularly brake tests, was pretty violent.

Some of the coaches, like the trucks, were put out on site test (loaned to operators) for normal use and appraisal. When one of these came in briefly needing investigation of a complaint, a quick way to provide a load was to grab any available workshop fitters or engineers; all of who welcomed the chance to skive off proper work and give the test driver a hard time.

The Chief Engineer had decreed that Commercial Vehicle Engineers must learn to drive coaches and trucks. This was fine for making them understand the weaknesses of their design, but a bit expensive accident-wise. I was on board a VAL with a brand new body driven by an engineer who ripped out the entire side on a gatepost entering the factory after a test run. Traffic island bollards were wiped out repeatedly at the bottom of Cutenhoe, the first tight right turn on the test route! Not all the engineers were as bad as this, in fact most of them became highly skilled PSV and truck drivers. All coaches had to pass an annual PSV inspection by the Ministry that included a cleanliness check, and if the inspector could whack the seats and get dust to rise, the vehicle failed.

As Superintendent of the Experimental Workshops, I had to get the coach prepared and put a couple of labourers to unload it and to get to work with beaters to get the dust out. It could take all day. But to make really sure, we parked the coach where the sun wouldn't reach it so any rising dust was harder to spot.

One time we had a lot of coach operators in to look at a new model, I think it was the VAM. I was one of the demonstration drivers, and we gave them a good long ride before taking them to lunch at a restaurant near Dunstable; this had a very tight, difficult entrance, most certainly not one intended to take coaches. Having built the chassis with an Eaton two-speed axle, I had developed a habit of doing split changes with the gearbox and axle during testing. Halfway round the route the vehicle proved my theory that it was possible to get an artificial neutral where the prop-shaft could spin on it's own. I managed to get it to take up the drive again and thought what a prat I was to let it do this during a demonstration. However, these grisly old operators from 'oop North' (who I expected to be highly critical of cheap Bedford coaches) patted me on the back for my driving and were very complimentary about the coach! And that was before their liquid lunch!'

Top Right: *The development of a new product was often years ahead of its commercial release, and this is perhaps a good example of a body-styling fitting into that category. This picture is taken in 1975 in Morocco as the YRT carries an experimental Duple Goldliner body. The side panel carries a Bedford/GM/Duple logo, and the headboard states Goldliner, but this model of body was not introduced into the UK until 1981. It even includes rear screen wipers. As a matter of interest JKX 742N heads to Ouarzazate (the capital of the province) from Ait Ben Haddou. The small town it has just visited is now largely deserted but it features some fascinating high-rise dwellings made completely of clay and straw.*

Middle Right: *Not all test runs took Bedford engineers to exotic places like the UNESCO heritage site mentioned above - a little more mundane, is the testing of Plaxton-bodied BXE 246J from the experimental fleet on the Vauxhall proving ground at Millbrook.*

Bottom Right: *The MkII Duple Dominant / YRT Demonstrator, OWA 998R, driven by Bedford engineers in the winter of 1976/7 - note the side panel livery.* Duple Motors

The words of the song, 'We are keeping the dream alive' could be well applied to the annual Bedford Gathering, held each August in Cambridgeshire. Here organiser Richard Haughey looks on as a Manchester-registered Bedford OB - Duple Vista C29F (LNA 367) drives out from the rally site loaned by Dews of Somersham in August 2000. Alan Earnshaw   for details check out www.bg-event.co.uk

This series of books has been a real trip down memory lane, for the authors and we hope that this has come across in your reading of the three titles. As series editor I have been undoubtedly assisted by the efforts of a large number of people over the past three years, but especially Mike Berry, Martin Eltham and at the last minute Andrew Webster.

Between us we have made quite a few telephone calls to former colleagues, operators and enthusiasts who we knew could assist with this project. All willingly helped with information and advice, although sadly these are too numerous to mention, but those who contributed know that our thanks are expressed all the same.

There are a number of people to whom we owe special thanks, namely: -

Anglco Ltd., Batley
Bailey's Coachbuilders, Bidulph
The Bedford Bus & Coach Register
Robert W. Berry,
Jeff Colledge
Eaton Transmissions Ltd.
Phill Green
Barry Harvey
Stuart Harris, Vauxhall Motors
Richard Haughey
Malcolm Knight
David Macilroy
Marshalls of Cambridge
Martin Perry, Wacton Coach Sales
Plaxtons Ltd.
Reeve Burgess Ltd.
Matthew Richardson,
Salopia Coaches, Wem
Dennis Sherer, Vauxhall Motors
Gary Smith, De-Luxe, New Zealand
Soc. of Motor Manufacturers & Traders
Peter Stone, Vauxhall Motors
Leo Taylor
Andrew Webster
White's Coaches
Malcolm Wright, Roadmaster
Wrights of Ballymena,

Finally the book is offered in memory of
SUE HAUGHEY
who sadly lost her long battle against illness during the production of this book.